D1474378

Human Centered Design Toolkit
2nd Edition

ISBN: 978-0-9846457-0-1 (sc)

First published by IDEO 5/13/2011

Printed in Canada

HUMAN CENTERED DESIGN

TOOLKIT

2ND EDITION

WATER STORAGE AND TRANSPORTATION, INDIA

INCREASING FARMER INCOMES, CAMBODIA

ENCOURAGING TECHNOLOGY ADOPTION, KENYA

TABLE OF CONTENTS

CREATE

The Create section will help you translate what you learned in the field into concrete solutions.

DELIVER

The Deliver section will give you the tools to go from ideas and prototypes to solutions and plans that can be implemented. It will also help you create a learning plan to measure and continue iterating on your designs.

The Field Guide contains worksheets that will help you to prepare for and conduct field research. The Field Guide and the Aspirations Cards, are all you will need to take to the field with you.

AN
INTRO
DUCTI
ONAN
INTRO

ARE YOU LOOKING TO...

Bring innovation to the base of the pyramid? Enter a new region? Adapt a technology to your region? Understand the needs of constituents better? Find new methods for monitoring and evaluation?

THIS TOOLKIT WAS MADE FOR YOU.

It contains the elements to Human-Centered Design, a process used for decades to create new solutions for multi-national corporations. This process has created ideas such as the HeartStart defibrillator, CleanWell natural antibacterial products, and the Blood Donor System for the Red Cross—innovations that have enhanced the lives of millions of people.

Now Human-Centered Design can help you enhance the lives of people living on less than $2/day.

This process has been specially-adapted for organizations like yours that work with communities in need in Africa, Asia, and Latin America.

Human-Centered Design (HCD) will help you **hear** the needs of constituents in new ways, **create** innovative solutions to meet these needs, and **deliver** solutions with financial sustainability in mind.

LET'S GET STARTED.

WHY DO HUMAN CENTERED DESIGN?

Because it can help your organization connect better with the people you serve. It can transform data into actionable ideas. It can help you to see new opportunities. It can help to increase the speed and effectiveness of creating new solutions.

We are excited about our ability to continue replicating the Human-Centered Design process to create and bring to scale new approaches to provide eye care in the developing world.

—VISIONSPRING, INDIA

HCD surprised us because even people who didn't know a lot about the topic were able to create so many solutions.

—IDE VIETNAM

WHY A TOOLKIT?

Because the people are the experts.

They are the ones who know best what the right solutions are. This kit doesn't offer solutions. Instead, it offers techniques, methods, tips, and worksheets to guide you through a process that gives voice to communities and allows their desires to guide the creation and implementation of solutions.

Because only you know how to best use it.

Human-Centered Design is a process broken into a set of tools. This is so that you can pick and choose which techniques work best for your context and your situation. Use it alone or along with PRISM, value chain analysis, PRA, triangulation or other methods you use in your organization to imagine and implement new ideas.

THE THREE LENSES OF HUMAN-CENTERED DESIGN

Human-Centered Design (HCD) is a process and a set of techniques used to create new solutions for the world. Solutions include products, services, environments, organizations, and modes of interaction.

The reason this process is called "human-centered" is because it starts with the people we are designing for. The HCD process begins by examining the needs, dreams, and behaviors of the people we want to affect with our solutions. We seek to listen to and understand what they want. We call this the Desirability lens. We view the world through this lens throughout the design process.

Once we have identified a range of what is Desirable, we begin to view our solutions through the lenses of Feasibility and Viability. We carefully bring in these lenses during the later phases of the process.

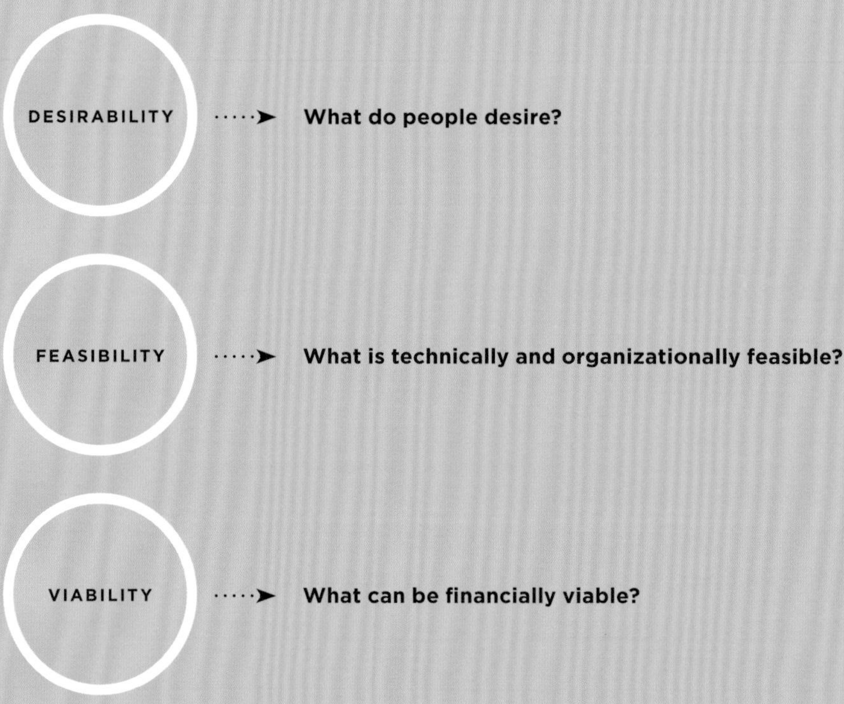
DESIRABILITY
What do people desire?
FEASIBILITY
What is technically and organizationally feasible?
VIABILITY
What can be financially viable?

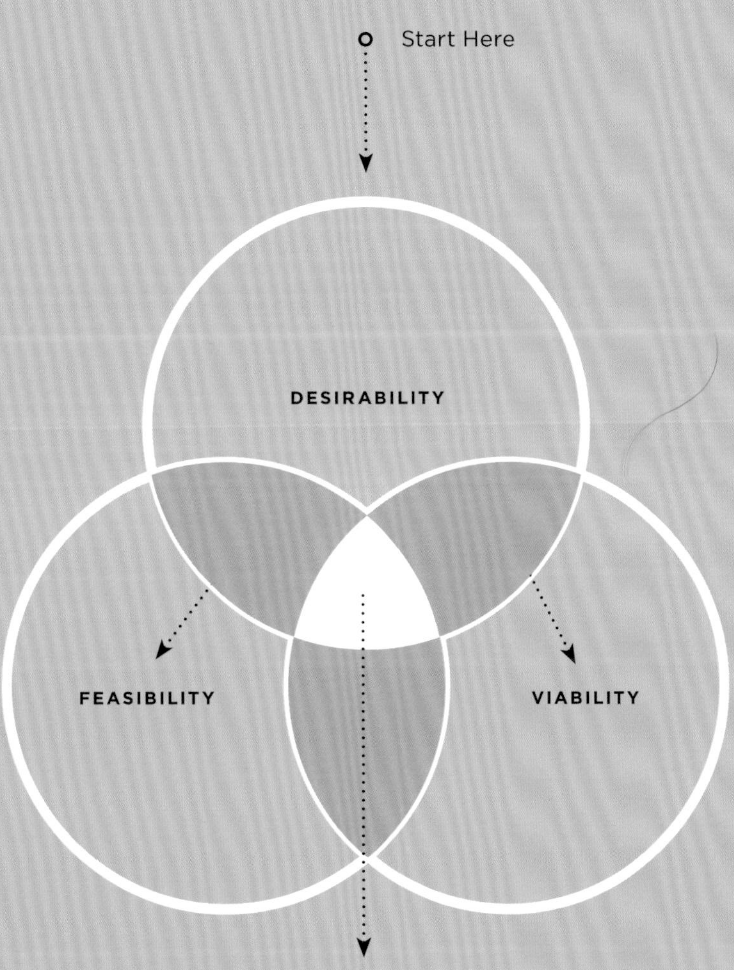

The solutions that emerge at the end of the Human-Centered Design should hit the overlap of these three lenses; they need to be **Desirable, Feasible, and Viable.**

THE HCD PROCESS

The process of Human-Centered Design starts with a specific Design Challenge and goes through three main phases: Hear, Create, and Deliver. The process will move your team from concrete observations about people, to abstract thinking as you uncover insights and themes, then back to the concrete with tangible solutions.

HEAR

During the Hear phase, your Design Team will collect stories and inspiration from people. You will prepare for and conduct field research.

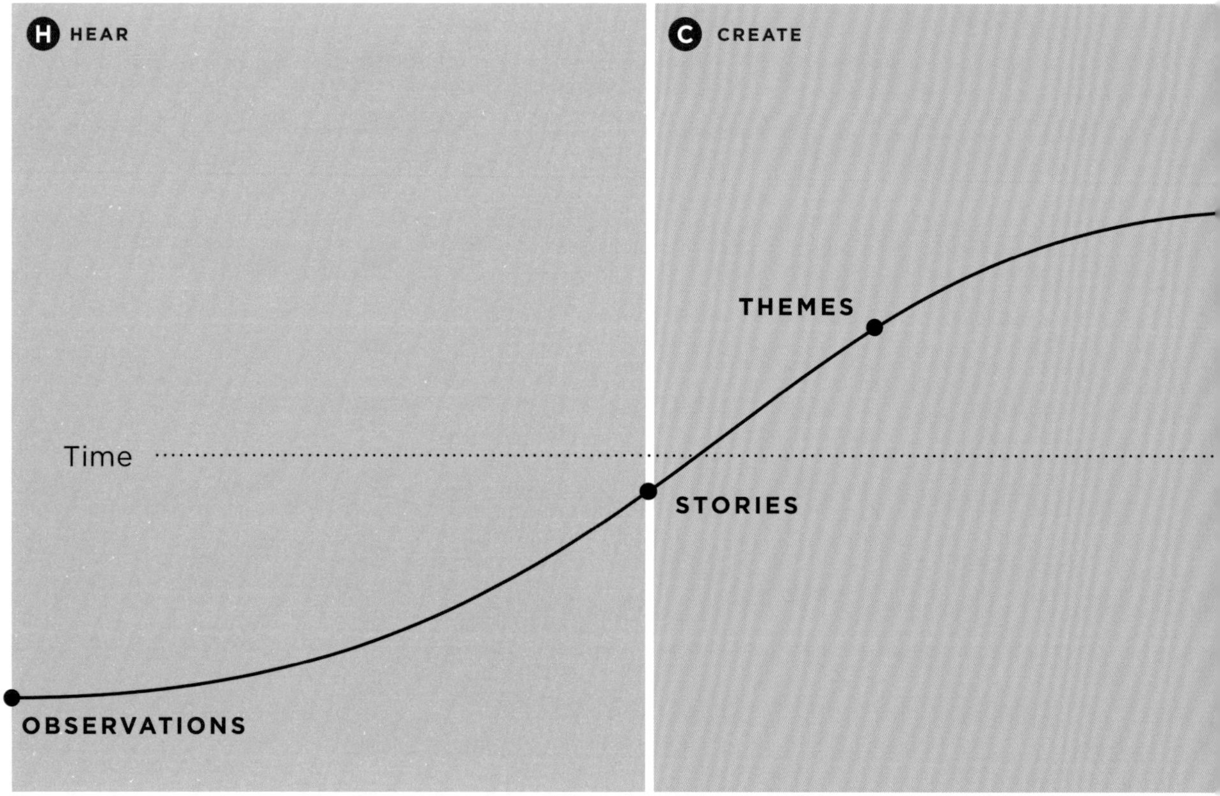

CREATE

In the Create phase, you will work together in a workshop format to translate what you heard from people into frameworks, opportunities, solutions, and prototypes. During this phase you will move together from concrete to more abstract thinking in identifying themes and opportunities, and then back to the concrete with solutions and prototypes.

DELIVER

The Deliver phase will begin to realize your solutions through rapid revenue and cost modeling, capability assessment, and implementation planning. This will help you launch new solutions into the world.

D DELIVER

Abstract

OPPORTUNITIES

SOLUTIONS

PROTOTYPES

Concrete

IMPLEMENTATION PLAN

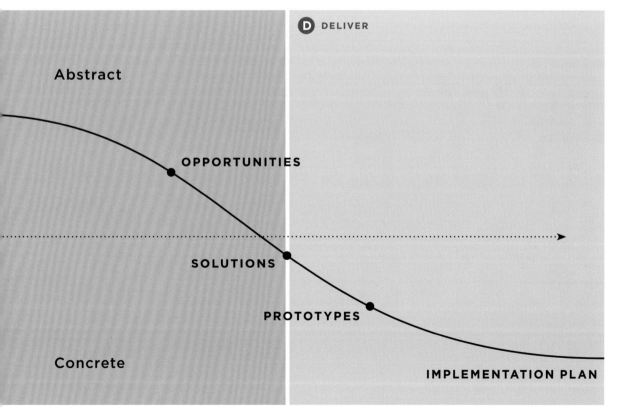

To recall these phases, simply remember H-C-D.

HOW TO USE THIS TOOLKIT

This toolkit will guide you through an innovation process based on HCD methodology.

A FLEXIBLE TOOLKIT

Using this toolkit on its own will yield great solutions. However, HCD is also very flexible and can complement or be supplemented by various other approaches. Methods such as Participatory Rural Appraisal (PRA), Subsector/Value Chain Analysis and Triangulation can all be incorporated into the HCD methodology provided here. For example, your Design Challenge may necessitate knowing about the mapping of village resources. If a team member is familiar with a PRA method effective for gathering this kind of information, it should absolutely be incorporated into the process.

So be creative and rigorous in choosing and mixing your methods – the best outcomes might come from the most unexpected combinations!

TIP

There is the “facilitator” version of the Toolkit. If you are the facilitator, use the notes provided to you in the margins as rough instructions of how to move your team forward through the innovation process. Please add any additional instructions, methods, or techniques you feel would be relevant to your design challenge.

WATCH OUT

The facilitator must user his/her power wisely. The facilitator is a role to lead the team through the process; this person can certainly contribute to the content of the ideas, but should not use his/her power to sway decisions.

BEST PRACTICES FOR INNOVATION

By completing thousands of innovation and design challenges, IDEO has learned a few rules for creating an environment to facilitate innovation. See if any of these can be applied to your organization.

MULTI-DISCIPLINARY TEAMS

The challenges you face are very complex and are likely to have been explored by predecessors. You will have a higher likelihood of success at solving such complex, difficult, and already-examined problems by intentionally assembling the right team of people. This team will work best if it consists of a core group of 3-8 individuals, one of whom is the facilitator. By mixing different disciplinary and educational backgrounds, you will have a better chance of coming up with unexpected solutions when these people approach problems from different points of view.

DEDICATED SPACES

Having a separate project space allows the team to be constantly inspired by imagery from the field, immersed in their post-it notes, and able to track the progress of the project. If possible, find a dedicated space for your design team to focus on the challenge.

FINITE TIMEFRAMES

Many people notice that they work best with deadlines and concrete timelines. Likewise, an innovation project with a beginning, middle, and end is more likely to keep the team motivated and focused on moving forward.

TIP

To ensure that there is a balanced gender perspective, involve female staff in all phases of this process.

SCENARIOS OF USE

The following Scenarios of Use help to outline four possible ways to use this toolkit for innovation. The first two scenarios utilize the principle of finite timeframes to frame the entire challenge, while the latter two demonstrate how small sections of the toolkit can be used to provide motivation, concrete goals, and a path to getting unstuck in longer-term programs.

SCENARIO 1: THE WEEK-LONG DEEP DIVE

This mode of engagement forces the design team to work quickly to gather and analyze data, then moves rapidly to solutions, prototypes and plans. The one-week timeframe is a familiar timeline that is long enough to gain good understanding, yet short enough to allow a stressed organization to put limited resources against a challenge. This format is good for early-phase learning and for spurring new thinking.

Use When You:

» Need to learn about a new area or challenge quickly.
» Need to kick-start thinking about a long-standing intractable problem.
» Want to refresh the thinking of the staff.

Pull Out and Use:

» All sections of the Toolkit in sequence.

TIP

Know the limitations of your data and your early prototypes when doing a Week-Long Deep Dive. If validity is necessary without much time for research, use secondary data to triangulate your findings. Build a plan for iterating early prototypes for future refinement.

SCENARIO 2: THE SEVERAL-MONTH DEEP DIVE

A longer Deep Dive can last several weeks to several months. This mode of use enables a deeper, more nuanced understanding and theorization of a complex challenge or problem. With a longer time frame, more locations can be examined and more stakeholders in the value chain can become participants in the process.

Use When You:

» Need to design robust solutions because the funds for implementation are available.

» Have the resources to allocate on thinking through a multi-faceted challenge.

» Need to engage many actors in the process, such as partners, value chain stakeholders, funders, etc.

Pull Out and Use:

» All sections of the Toolkit, allowing the nature of the Challenge to dictate the appropriate timeframes for each Phase.

TIP

When you have more time for a Deep Dive, it may be tempting to spend the vast majority of time doing more research. Pay attention and notice when you are hitting decreasing returns and stop the research when you are learning little new information. Remember—in the early stages, you are doing research to understand the problem and inspire the team. There will be time to validate later.

SCENARIO 3:
ACTIVATING ALREADY-EXISTING KNOWLEDGE

Often organizations have a great deal of research and already-existing information but are unable to translate all that information into actionable solutions. In this case, the processes outlined in Create and Deliver can help your team transform what you know into things you can start doing.

Use When You:

» Have a lot of data and you don't quite know what to do with it.
» Have been hearing interesting stories from the field staff and want to see if those stories can yield new opportunities or solutions.
» Have a robust research methodology that you like better than the one in this toolkit.

Pull Out and Use:

» Create
» Deliver

TIP

Even if you have the information captured in a different form (in Word documents, for example), take the time to translate that information through the Story Sharing methods outlined in the first part of the Create booklet.

SCENARIO 4: COMPLEMENTING EXISTING LONG-TERM ACTIVITIES

Many HCD methods are applicable at different times to the challenges your organization will face in Technology Adaptation, Monitoring & Evaluation, etc. We hope that you will find some of the techniques useful in infusing the spirit of innovation in your day-to-day activities, even when there is no explicit Design Challenge at hand. Pick and choose your methods as you wish to help complement your daily work.

Use When You:

» Want a new technique to add to your work routines.
» See a method in this toolkit that you find applicable to the daily challenges you face.
» Can't set aside the resources for an HCD project, but want to infuse the spirit of Human-Centered Design in your everyday work.

Pull Out and Use:

» Any pieces of your choosing.

TIP

For example, if you're working on adapting an existing technology and have already-existing information about the context you want to adapt to, use Steps 3, 4, 5, and 6 in the Create book to guide you through several iterations of opportunity identification, brainstorming, prototyping, and user feedback.

On the other hand, if you are looking for help in gathering data for M&E reporting, use the exercises in the Field Guide to supplement your current activities.

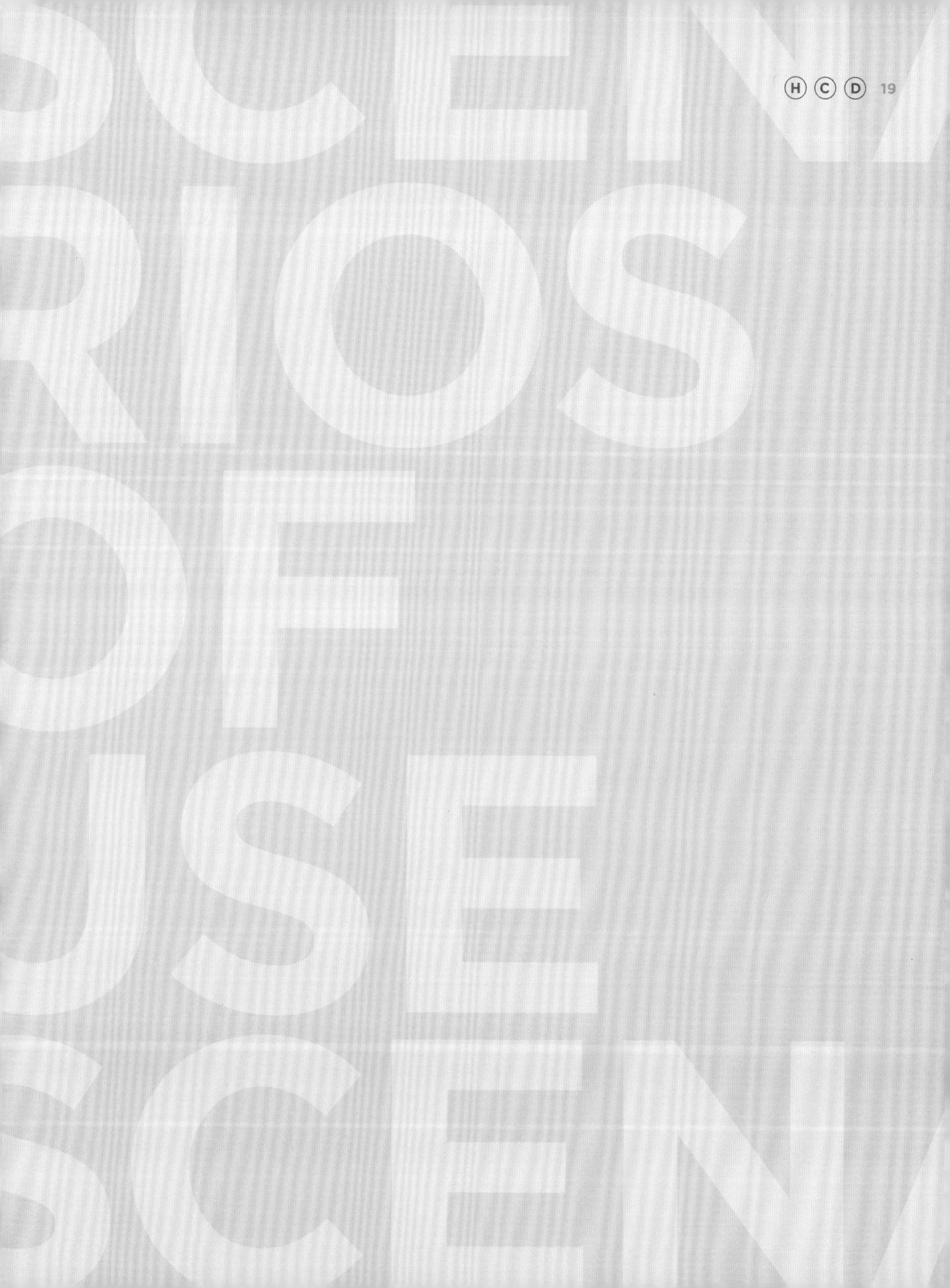
SCEN
RIOS
OF
USE
SCEN

HEAR

IMPROVING ACCESS TO ECONOMIC RESOURCES, MONGOLIA

AGATABO
Koresha ak atabo ushuhanye
ibintu wunva bikenewe kandi
byateza imbere akarere utuyemo.

IBYAWE GUSA
Koresha amafaranga ari muri
iy'ibahasha kugura ikintu ushaka.
Nugera ku ifoto ya cyumi
nagatandatu, fotora ikintu waguze
amafaranga wahawe.

WATER STORAGE AND TRANSPORTATION, INDIA

HEAR: GOALS

Designing meaningful and innovative solutions that serve your constituents begins with understanding their needs, hopes and aspirations for the future.

The Hear booklet will equip the team with methodologies and tips for engaging people in their own contexts in order to understand the issues at a deep level.

Goals of this book are to guide:

» WHO TO TALK TO
» HOW TO GAIN EMPATHY
» HOW TO CAPTURE STORIES

“”

Great technique for getting farmers to tell stories.

—IDE ZAMBIA

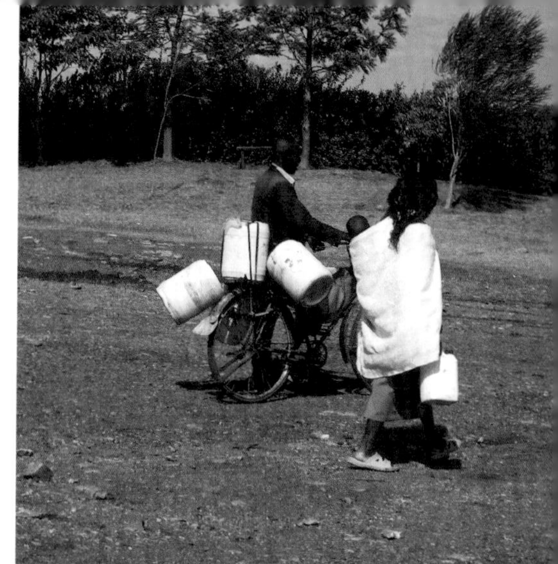

HEAR: OUTPUTS

At the end of the Hear section, prepare to go to the field by completing these worksheets from the Field Guide:

Recruiting Plan
Research Schedule
Identity, Power & Politics
Group Interview Guide
Individual Interview Guide

Outputs of the Hear Phase are:

- **» PEOPLES' STORIES**
- **» OBSERVATIONS OF CONSTITUENTS' REALITY**
- **» DEEPER UNDERSTANDING OF NEEDS, BARRIERS, & CONSTRAINTS**

Qualitative research methods enable the design team to develop deep empathy for people they are designing for, to question assumptions, and to inspire new solutions. At the early stages of the process, research is generative — used to inspire imagination and inform intuition about new opportunities and ideas. In later phases, these methods can be evaluative—used to learn quickly about people's response to ideas and proposed solutions.

HEAR: THEORY

What will qualitative research methods do?

Qualitative methods can uncover deeply-held needs, desires, and aspirations. It is particularly useful in early-stage research to test assumptions about the world, and when we cannot assume that the researchers already know the entire universe of possible answers, beliefs, and ideas of the participants.

Qualitative methods can help unveil people's social, political, economic, and cultural opportunities and barriers in their own words.

Qualitative research can also be powerful for analyzing and mapping the relational dynamics between people, places, objects, and institutions. This is possible because phenomena in the social world tend to be internally related (that is, they are mutually-dependent and co-constituted).

By examining the extreme ends of a set of phenomena in depth, the entire universe of relationships can be illuminated since other instances will fall somewhere on the map of relations and links. Once a set of relationships are identified, they can be interrogated using interpretive methods or further refined for quantitative testing.

What will qualitative research methods not do?

Qualitative methods will not determine "average" behaviors/attitudes or answer questions such as: "Are people in X region more likely to do this than in Y region?" This is because qualitative methods do not cover a sample large enough to be statistically significant.

Deep understanding, not broad coverage, is the strength of qualitative research.

In later phases of the design process, quantitative research becomes a good complement to understand, for example, the potential adoption of a new solution or to understand how the effect of solutions will vary from region to region.

Facilitator Notes

Time:
1-1.5 Hours

Difficulty:
★★★★★

Step 1: Work with leadership to identify a list of criteria for the challenge. (i.e. Does it need to fit into a certain timeframe? Does it need to have a geographical or topical focus? Does it need to fit into an existing initiative? Does it need to explore new opportunities?)

Step 2: With leadership, the design team, and/or constituents, make a list of the challenges you are facing.

Step 3: Re-frame those challenges from the constituent's point of view and broader context.

Step 4: Vote or select the top two or three challenges based on your criteria.

Step 5: Narrow to one challenge with input from key stakeholders.

Step 6: Write a succinct, one sentence Design Challenge to guide the design team.

IDENTIFY A DESIGN CHALLENGE

The foundation of HCD is a concise Design Challenge. This challenge will guide the questions you will ask in the field research and the opportunities and solutions you will develop later in the process. A Design Challenge is phrased in a human-centered way with a sense of possibility. For example: "Create savings and investment products that are appropriate for people living in rural areas."

TIP #1

The Design Challenge can be decided by organizational leadership or can be developed through a team-based approach. In either case, begin by identifying challenges people are facing or springboard off opportunities the organization is interested in exploring. Narrow this list down to one specific design challenge.

TIP #2

A good Design Challenge should be:

» Framed in human terms (rather than technology, product, or service functionality)

» Broad enough to allow you to discover the areas of unexpected value

» Narrow enough to make the topic manageable

WATCH OUT

The challenge you choose may be related to adoption of new technologies, behaviors, medicines, products, or services. This might lead to framing a design challenge that is organization-focused, such as "How can we get people in villages to adopt savings accounts?" Instead, to act as a springboard for innovation, the challenge should be re-framed in a more human-centered way, such as "How can we create a financial safety net for people in villages?"

TRY

Start the design challenge with an action verb such as "Create", "Define", "Adapt", etc. Or phrase the challenge as a question starting with: "How can...?"

WHAT MAKES PEOPLE SAY 'YES'

...ST HARVEST ...ECHNOLOGY (FRUIT-DRYING)

income opps beyond agr.

what ris... mgmt pr... do farmer... need...

...CHNOLOGIES ...HAT SERVE .../DAY + ...20/30/DAY

Minimize crop production costs

LINKS TO MICROFINA... INSTITUT...

...st channel facilitate ...mer outputs

How can we compete with motor pumps?

Coordina... syste...

How do farmers think about risk mgmt?

Separate bad treadle pump history from our

SEE... CHA...

STEP 1

CASE STUDY

TEAM-BASED DESIGN CHALLENGE DEFINITION

In Ethiopia, IDE defined the design challenge through a series of different steps. First a small core team - the country director and IDE corporate staff — determined a set of criteria and short list of important challenges.

Armed with this information, the country director and design team developed a set of criteria for the design challenge. This criteria was:

» Limited enough to complete the challenge in 3-4 days

» Focused on farmer needs

» Broad enough to discover what is desirable to farmers

Next, the team listed all the challenges they wanted to pursue. The country director then gave the team some information about the conversation among the core team which helped to focus the choices. Referring back to the criteria the team developed, the challenges were narrowed through a democratic vote. The top three were:

» What can we offer farmers who don't have enough rainwater access?

» What are the best ways to communicate IDE offerings to farmers?

» What makes farmers say yes?

The team discussed the possibilities and decided that the second and third were actually closely related. So the team re-phrased the Design Challenge to become: "Define the appropriate approach for reaching a larger number of smallholder farmers with IDE offerings."

After more discussion and a final vote, this challenge was selected.

RECO
NIZE
KNOW
LEDG
RECO

RECOGNIZE EXISTING KNOWLEDGE

Chances are good that you already have some knowledge about the topic. Conducting a "What Do We Know?" session helps call forth existing knowledge related to the Design Challenge. Once documented, you can freely focus on discovering what you don't yet know.

TRY

First, on Post-Its, write down what you already know about the Design Challenge, including:

» What people need or want

» What technologies can help in this challenge

» What solutions or ideas are being tried in other areas

» Any early hypotheses about how to solve the Design Challenge

Are there any contradictions or tensions that emerge? Where is the team's knowledge the strongest: on the needs of people, on the technological possibilities, or in how to implement ideas?

Next, write down what you don't know but need to learn about the area of investigation, such as:

» What constituents do, think, or feel

» How people value offerings

» What constituents' future needs may be

» Challenges to implementation of ideas

Where are the biggest needs for research?
How should the recruiting strategy be tailored?
Which categories might structure the discussion guide?

Facilitator Notes

Time:
30-60 mins.

Difficulty:
★★★☆☆

Step 1: Post the design challenge so that the team can see it.

Step 2: Hand out post-it notes to the design team, and ask them to write what they already know about the topic. Have one piece of information per post-it note.

Step 3: Ask each person to read their notes, and post them under the design challenge. Ask others to disagree or challenge any of the assumptions that come out.

Step 4: Ask the team to write down on post-it notes what they don't know about the challenge and read their notes. Post these notes in a different area.

Step 5: Group the post-it notes into themes to help the team develop research methods, a recruiting plan, and the interview guide.

IDENTIFY PEOPLE TO SPEAK WITH

Recruiting appropriate and inspirational participants is critical. Attention to gender, ethnicity, and class balance is crucial for research.

For research meant to inspire new opportunities, it is useful to find people who represent "extremes." Extreme participants help to unearth unarticulated behaviors, desires, and needs of the rest of the population, but are easier to observe and identify because they feel the effects more powerfully than others. By including both ends of your spectrum as well as some people in the middle, the full range of behaviors, beliefs, and perspectives will be heard even with a small number of participants. Including this full range will be important in the later phases, especially in constructing good frameworks and providing inspiration for brainstorming.

GENDER

Some communities may be resistant to male NGO staff interviewing women. Make sure female staff help recruit & interview women.

WATCH OUT

Group sessions are a great springboard to identify participants for the individual interviews. However, communities often want to showcase only the most successful constituents or male community members to NGOs.

Facilitator Notes

Time:
30-60 mins.

Difficulty:
★★★☆☆

Step 1: Develop the spectrum along which to recruit. Generate several options (i.e. High income to low income, early adopter to risk averse, large landholder to landless). Individually or collectively narrow to one or two relevant spectrums to make sure "extremes" are covered in the research.

Step 2: Identify the relevant locations to recruit participants. Ask stakeholders to list good areas for this research. Pick 2-5 field sites that vary from one another (i.e. a dry and a wet site or a site in a central district and one more remote).

Step 3: Select appropriate community contacts to help arrange community meetings and individual interviews. Make sure community contacts include men & women.

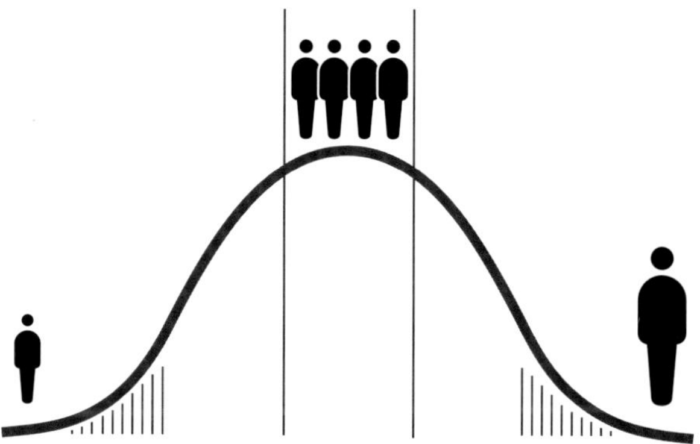

TIP #1

One-third of participants might be "ideal constituents": those who are successful, adopt new technologies quickly, and/or exhibit desirable behaviors.

One-third of participants should be on the opposite extreme: those who are very poor, resistant to new technologies, and/or exhibit problematic behaviors.

One-third of participants should be somewhere in between: those who the researchers believe represent more "average" people.

TIP #2

To satisfy the economic spectrum from the more well off to the very poor, you might ask:

» "Can you introduce me to a family who cannot afford to send their children to school?"

» "Who has not been able to afford maintenance or repairs to their home?"

» "Who has experienced a recent setback (medical problems, bad harvest, etc)?"

Refer to the Field Guide to help guide your recruiting.

CHOOSE RESEARCH METHODS

Design research is useful to not only understand individuals but also frame individual behaviors in the context and community that surrounds them. Therefore, it will be important to employ many methods of research. In addition to the methods described in this book, secondary sources and quantitative data can be supplemented to understand income or asset variances across different regions. Five methods described here are:

» Individual Interview
» Group Interview
» In Context Immersion
» Self-Documentation
» Community-Driven Discovery
» Expert Interviews
» Seeking Inspiration in New Places

METHOD: INDIVIDUAL INTERVIEW

Facilitator Notes

Time: 60-90 mins.

Difficulty: ★★☆☆☆

Step 1: After your team has written the Interview Guide (see Field Guide), practice the individual interview by partnering in teams of two. One person plays the role of the interviewer and the other the interviewee. Ask the teams to go through a "practice interview" with their partner.

Step 2: Ask the team what they learned through this exercise. Are there any topics or questions that are missing?

Individual interviews are critical to most design research, since they enable a deep and rich view into the behaviors, reasoning, and lives of people. If possible, arrange to meet the participant at his/her home or workplace, so you can see them in context. In-context interviews give the participant greater ease and allow you to see the objects, spaces, and people that they talk about during the interview.

WATCH OUT

If there are many people on the research team, no more than three people should attend any single interview so as to not overwhelm the participant and/or create difficulty in accommodating a large group inside the participant's home.

Refer to Step 5: Develop an Interview Approach to create a set of questions for your individual interviews.

TIP #1

The interview should be conducted without an audience, since the presence of neighbors, friends, or others can sway what the person says or what they are able to reveal. Privacy can often be difficult to create, however. One tactic to accomplish privacy is to have one person on the research team pull the audience aside and engage them in a parallel conversation in a place where the primary interview cannot be heard.

TIP #2

Assign the following roles so that each person has a clear purpose visible to the participant:

- one person to lead the interview
- a note taker
- a photographer

METHOD: GROUP INTERVIEW

Group-based interviews can be a valuable way to learn about a community quickly. Group interviews can be good for learning about community life and dynamics, understanding general community issues, and giving everyone in a community the chance to voice their views.

Group interviews are not good for gaining a deep understanding of individual income streams, uncovering what people really think, or understanding how to change commonly-held beliefs or behaviors.

TIP #1

Guidelines for group meetings:
Size: 7-10 people from diverse economic backgrounds

Place: Meet on neutral ground in a shared community space that all people have access to (regardless of age, gender, status, race).

Gender: Mixed or same-sex groups depending on the customs in that community (if men and women should meet separately, two facilitators can run the groups in parallel).

Age: Mixed groups of parents and teens/children, depending on the topic and local context.

WATCH OUT

Are the viewpoints of men and women equally valued in this community? If not, it may make sense to have two meetings, one with women only and one with men only.

Are political heavyweights (such as chiefs, local administrators, etc) present? If so, their opinions may hamper the ability of others to speak freely.

Does the community view you as a source of funds, gifts, or charity? If so, their interactions may be influenced by the desire to access potential benefits; it may be helpful to prepare an introduction that makes the purpose of the interview clear and state that nothing will be given away.

Facilitator Notes

Time:
1.5-2 Hours

Difficulty:
★★★☆☆

Step 1: After the team develops a Group Interview Guide (see Step 4), have the team partner in groups of two for a practice interview. Ask the interviewers to develop an approach for including women and quieter members of the group. Ask them also to develop strategies for asking people who may be dominating the conversation to allow other people to answer.

Step 2: Have the team share "best practices" for including quieter members of the group and redirecting the conversation away from people who are dominating the conversation.

TIP #2

NGOs can sometimes unintentionally send a message of separateness by wearing branded NGO clothing and creating spatial distance between themselves and the participants. It's important to lessen these barriers and to disrupt common hierarchical perceptions of benefactor/researcher and recipient/participant. Here are some tips:

» Sit at the same height level as the participants

» If there is more than one researcher, don't sit together; stagger yourselves throughout the group

» Try not to wear organization-branded clothing that signifies your status as benefactor or researcher

» Emulate the same status of clothing as participants (note: this does not mean wearing the "traditional dress" of the constituent community if this is not your own heritage)

Refer to Step 5 : Develop an Interview Approach to identify questions for the group.

METHOD: IN CONTEXT IMMERSION

Meeting people where they live, work, and socialize and immersing yourself in their context reveals new insights and unexpected opportunities.

Human-Centered Design works best when the designers understand the people they are designing for not just on an intellectual level, but also on an experiential level. Try to do what your constituents do and talk to them about their experience of life in the moment.

Facilitator Notes

Time:
2-4 Days

Difficulty:
★★★★☆

Step 1: To plan a homestay, identify people willing to host a researcher for one-to-three nights in their home. Depending on local customs, level of safety, and language barriers, team members can stay in homes individually or partner up in groups of two to three people.

Step 2: Make sure the team understands that the goal of this exercise is to see how participants live day-to-day. Advise your team not to bring elaborate gifts, food, or alcohol to the homestay. However, a small gift of ordinary household supplies or help with normal family expenses is perfectly fine.

Step 3: Tell team members to participate with the family in their normal routines. Ask the team to spend time with and talk to the men, women, and children in the household. It's important to see how the household works from all these different perspectives.

GENDER

On a project in rural India, people said that cultural tradition prevented women from touching men who are not immediate family members. However, by spending several days in a village, the team observed that there were many instances in which trained or uniformed women doing specific jobs were able to touch men without any serious problems. These gaps between what people say and what they do are not bad. In fact, seeing these differences may highlight new opportunities; for example, designing a new medical service that could be provided by uniformed women.

TRY #1

Work Alongside
Spend a few hours to a few days working with someone. By experiencing the business and activity firsthand, you may gain better understanding of their needs, barriers, and constraints.

TRY #2

Family Homestay
Ask a family to host 1-2 team members for a few nights in their home. Staying for a few nights allows the family to gain comfort and act naturally. After the second night, very few people can maintain a "show" for guests, and the understanding and empathy the team will gain will increase the longer you stay in one place.

TIP #1

What people say (and think) they do and what they actually do are not always the same thing.
With no intent to mislead you, people often have strong beliefs about what they do on a daily basis that differs from what they actually do. The goal is not to correct or point out the misperception, but rather to understand the difference.

TIP #2

Putting yourself in someone's shoes enables you to get beyond what people say to what they think and feel.
Being in-context means gaining true empathy through being with people in their real settings and doing the things they normally do. This kind of deep immersion gives us Informed Intuition that we take back with us to design solutions. We begin to take on the perspective of the interview participant which enables us to make design decisions with their perspective in mind.
Of course, we always go back into the field and get feedback from the source to see if our Informed Intuition led us to the right choices, and how we can improve them.

TIP #3

Deep immersion shows commitment and staying power.
For example, working with a person for a day in his or her field, living with a family for a few days or helping them bring their products to market are ways of showing your deep interest in the day-to-day lives of your participants. Trust is built over time and people feel at ease sharing their plans and hopes for the future. Many NGOs gain this depth of connection over many months of relationship building. Some techniques like the overnight stay described in the case study on the next page can accelerate this trust building.

12

CASE STUDY

OVERNIGHT STAY IN THE FIELD

On a project to increase small holder farmer income for IDE Ethiopia, **the design team stayed overnight in Arsi Negelle, Ethiopia, where they plowed the family's fields the next morning. The overnight enabled the team to get beyond the common stories people tell to NGOs and learn about one farmer's most intimate plans for the future.**

They visited a farmer named Roba the first evening and once again the next day.

When they first met Roba, he portrayed an overall sense of hopelessness. He described things that happened TO him, in particular the government's recent land redistribution. Some farmers received land in the irrigated area near the lake. Some did not. He was in the latter group.

The next day, he was shocked to discover that the team was still there. His demeanor had changed completely. He knew the team was committed. This time, he shared that in fact he did have a plan for pulling his family out of poverty. If he could secure a $200 USD loan, he would first buy an ox so he wouldn't have to trade two days of his own labor to borrow a neighbor's. Then he'd rent a piece of land in the irrigated territory and purchase improved seed. He no longer viewed the team as a wealthy NGO who was there to provide a free gift, but rather a partner in how he could take command of his own future.

METHOD: SELF-DOCUMENTATION

Self-Documentation is a powerful method for observing processes over a long period of time, or for understanding the nuances of community life when the researcher can't be there. Records of experiences, such as journal entries, allow the team to see how participants see their life, community, and relationships.

TRY

Recruit several people and give them cameras, video cameras, voice recorders or journals, with instructions. Ask them to document their experiences over a few days or weeks. Give participants instructions designed to guide them on how to easily record activities that will yield relevant information to the research project. The easier it is to self-document, the more likely it is that participants will complete the exercise.

TIP #1

Often teenagers and young people are good participants in self-documentary exercises. Young people tend to want to express themselves in new ways, and can find the process of documenting their lives and the community less intimidating than older adults.

TIP #2

You may find that your participants need a little help practicing the techniques for self-documentation. If this is the case, show some examples of how other people have done self-documentation, or spend a few hours with the participant to show them how to capture information.

GENDER

Be sensitive to who has access to what in a community. It is important to recruit both men and women in this exercise to have a balance of perspectives. Also be sensitive to class, age, and other factors that will affect the information people are able to collect and record.

Facilitator Notes

Time:
2-30 Days

Difficulty:
★★★☆☆

Step 1: Decide what you would like people to document -- their feelings, activities, family life, income, or behaviors. Based on this, decide what the best mode for collection of the information might be: photographs, diaries, voice recordings, etc.

Step 2: Give participants the tools and instructions to document themselves for several days.

Step 3: When you return to the participants, review the materials together. Remember to ask them not just what the things are that they documented, but also why they chose these details and how they felt about the items.

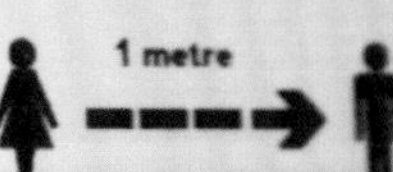
Each number shows you which picture you should take
LOOK HERE TO TAKE PICTURE
27-24. This is a picture of me (3)
23. This is in my pocket or purse
22. This is what I wear on my feet
21. This is where I live
20. This is where I work
19. This is where I sleep
18. This is what I see when I step outside
17. This is where I shop
16. This is what I bought for 500 francs
15. This is my favorite drink
14. This is my favorite food
13. You can only find this in my country
12. I wish I had this
11. I spend most of my time here
10. This is something I need
9. This is someone I love
8. This is where I relax
7. I spend time with friends here
6. This is someone I respect
5. This is beautiful to me
4. This is something I worry about
3. This is something I am proud of
2. This is something I want to improve
1. I use this every day
To advance film, turn wheel until it stops.
1 metre
Stand about two arms length from the person or thing you are shooting.

METHOD: COMMUNITY-DRIVEN DISCOVERY

In most cases, the real experts on a certain topic and those with the most insight for the Design Challenge are the people in the community or end customers. Consider recruiting members of the community to be the primary researchers, translators, designers and/or key informants for the project.

Community members with strong relationships, respected leaders, or people with a reputation for intelligence and fairness are often good people to identify as research partners. By asking people in the community to lead the research, the other participants may be able to express their concerns more openly and honestly. In addition, through their intimate knowledge of the community, these research partners can help interpret the hidden meaning and motivations behind the statements of other participants.

WATCH OUT

Community politics can sometimes transform a research project into a community battle for access to the resources of the researcher and/or NGO. Even when these resources are not real, the perception of favoritism can be damaging. Before starting a project utilizing community-driven discovery, it is important to understand the relevant dynamics and power relationships.

TRY

Find people in the community who are particularly innovative or who have been doing things out of the ordinary in order to achieve success. How might you partner with these individuals to inspire new solutions? What can be learned by leveraging their innovations and knowledge?

Facilitator Notes

Time: 2-4 Days

Difficulty: ★★★★☆

Step 1: Identify a few people in the community that will be good members to have on the design team. Try to ensure that these individuals are trusted and respected members of the community, that they are fair and unbiased, and have no personal stake in the results of the design solutions.

Step 2: Decide how you will compensate these individuals. Sometimes it will be appropriate to pay them a salary based on what other members of the design team are getting paid, while in other situations, non-monetary gifts are more appropriate. If you are uncertain, seek advice.

Step 3: Integrate these design team members at every point in the project, valuing their knowledge of the community dynamics and needs.

EXPER
RT INT
TER
VIEW
EXPER

METHOD: EXPERT INTERVIEWS

Experts can be called upon to provide in-depth and technical information. Reaching out to experts is particularly useful in cases where the team needs to learn a large amount of information in a short period of time, and/or where others have already done a lot of research on a topic.

Some examples of good times to call upon expert interviews are:

» To learn about the history of a particular community or topic

» To understand the regulations that might affect design and implementation of solutions

» To gather information about new technologies that have been recently invented or that are on the horizon

WATCH OUT

Expert interviews are not a substitute for primary research with participants and communities. Often experts overstate their expertise or develop their own assumptions and biases that can stifle innovation.

TIP #1

If possible, interview experts with different points of view on a topic in order to balance out biases.

TIP #2

Remember that the real experts are the people you're designing for. Don't ask experts for solutions or take their ideas as the final solution.

Facilitator Notes

Time:
1.5-3 hours

Difficulty:

Step 1: Identify the areas or topics that you would like to talk to experts about.

Step 2: Find and recruit these experts by telling them about your project and the intended length of time you will speak with them. Try to speak with people who have different opinions on the topics to challenge the team to think in new ways.

Step 3: Return to some of these experts during the Feedback portion of the project -- experts can be even more helpful when there is something tangible for them to respond to.

EMRI

METHOD: SEEK INSPIRATION IN NEW PLACES

One of the best ways to inspire new ideas is to look at similar experiences in other contexts, instead of focusing too narrowly on the research topic. The simple act of looking at different contexts can bring to mind new insights. For example a surgeon can get insights about organizing their medical supplies by visiting a hardware store, an airline employer might get ideas about check-in by observing a hotel front desk or a water-jug creator could observe other ways individuals transport heavy objects or liquids.

TRY #1

To identify inspirational settings, list all the distinct activities or emotions that make up the experience you are researching. For example, a doctor's visit might include the following activities and feelings: getting sick, discussing a doctor visit with family, travel, paying, and following doctor instructions such as taking medication or changing behavior. Find other situations that include some or all of these activities and then go and observe them.

TRY #2

This method is most useful when you have already done some research, and need to refresh your thinking.

Facilitator Notes

Time: 20-60 mins.

Difficulty: ★★★☆☆

Step 1: Think about all the activities, feelings, and behaviors that make up the experience of your challenge. Ask the team to list these together.

Step 2: Next to each activity, feeling, or behavior, write down a few other areas or situations where this exists. For example, if the activity is "use a device at the same time every day", other situations might be how people use alarm clocks, wells, or mobile phones.

Step 3: Have the team vote on the situations that they would like to observe for inspiration and arrange for an observation.

Step 4: During the observation, have the team take pictures and notes of the experience. Together, debrief on what this experience was like and what they can apply to the design challenge.

DEVELOP AN INTERVIEW APPROACH

Interviewing is an art that balances the dual needs of getting relevant information from the customer and engaging with them as a curious and empathetic friend. Intentionally developing your strategy for interviewing is key to managing this balance. Here we include three interview methods that may help you to develop the interview approach right for you:

» Interview Guide
» Sacrificial Concepts
» Interview Techniques

Facilitator Notes

Time:
1-2 Hours

Difficulty:
★★★★☆

Step 1: Generate a list of topics related to your design challenge to cover in field research.

Step 2: Sort the topics based on what are the main categories and sub-categories.

Step 3: Identify if any topics are specific to male or female activities.

Step 4: Break into groups of two. Take each main category and assign a group to generate a list of questions to ask in the field based on the topics listed in the main category.

Step 5: Have each group present their questions to the larger team and add any additional questions that may be missing.

METHOD: INTERVIEW GUIDE

The semi-structured interview is a key method of enabling dialogue and deep engagement with participants while retaining focus on a particular topic. Thoughtful structuring of the interview questions will take the participant on a mental journey from the specific to the aspirational to the tangible.

TIP #1

OPEN SPECIFIC
Warm up the participant with questions they are comfortable with.
1. Household demographics
2. Who does what in the household?
3. Stories of recent past

GO BROAD
Prompt bigger, even aspirational, thinking that they may not be accustomed to on a daily basis.
4. Aspirations for the future
5. System-based questions

PROBE DEEP
Dig deeper on the challenge at hand & prompt with 'what if' scenarios.
6. Income sources
7. Questions specific to innovation challenge
8. Sacrificial Concepts

TRY #1

Begin by brainstorming the topical areas you'd like to cover during the interviews, like

» sources of livelihood

» sources of information

» financing models

TRY #2

Use post-its to capture questions that respond to these topics. For 'sources of information,' one might ask:

» When you have a setback in your life, who do you go to for advice?

» Have you heard about new ways of doing things in the past year? How have you heard about them?

TRY #3

Move the post-its around to sort the questions into a logical flow based on the sequencing of START SPECIFIC, GO BROAD then PROBE DEEP.

Create your own in your Interview Guide at the back of your Field Guide based on the example on the opposite page.

METHOD: SACRIFICIAL CONCEPTS

Scenario-based questions or Sacrificial Concepts can help make hypothetical or abstract questions more accessible. A sacrificial concept is an idea or solution created to help understand the issue further. It is a concept that doesn't have to be feasible, viable, or possible since its only purpose is deeper understanding. A good sacrificial concept sparks a conversation, prompts a participant to be more specific in their stories, and helps check and challenge your assumptions.

Facilitator Notes

Time:
30-60 mins.

Difficulty:
★★★★☆

Step 1: Based on your Design Challenge, identify an abstract question you would like to know the answer to. Pose the abstract question to your partner, and note the response.

Step 2: Now turn the abstract question into a concrete scenario with two options. Pose your scenario-based question to your partner.

Step 3: Now change a few of the variables in your scenario and pose the question again.

What kinds of information did you learn from the different ways of questioning?

TIP

Abstract concepts difficult to answer for many people include:

» Questions about risk, insurance, and guarantees

» Questions about trade-offs

» Questions about return on investment

» Questions about future behavior

TRY #1

Make a question less abstract by creating a Sacrificial Concept:

Instead of asking: "How much would you pay to reduce the risk of purchasing new technology?"

Describe two scenarios for the participant to choose from: "If you had a choice between two new technologies that could improve your farm output. The first technology costs 1,000 and comes with no guarantee. The second costs 1,500 and comes with a guarantee that by the second harvest, your farm output will double or else we will come back, take the technology away, and give you back your 1,500. Which option would you prefer?" Discuss why.

TRY #2

Ask a person to compare your concept to the way they currently do things. You might also create two concepts that contrast with each other or are opposites. People have an easier time reacting to concepts if they have something to compare it to.

TRY #3

A sacrificial concept might be a scenario told verbally or shown in pictures or drawings. It might be an object that the person can handle. It might be an experience that a participant can try.

TRY #4

Look at your design challenge and your big questions. What topics do you want to explore deeply? Create a sacrificial concept to help you prompt the right conversation.

CASE STUDY

MOCK SHOPS IN RURAL GHANA

For a project on developing consumer goods franchises in Ghana, the IDEO team set up a Mock Shop in villages in order to understand how people make purchase decisions. The mock shop featured personal-care products from local and international brands at a range of price points.

In the shop, the team was able to observe people's decision-making processes in action. They saw how long a person stayed, observed the browsing process, heard common questions, and saw customers' processes for accessing the money needed to make a purchase.

After a participant looked through the shop and decided what to buy (or not to buy anything), the team asked follow-up questions about their decision. Why had they chosen to buy an item or not when looking at a product? What were they considering when looking at product X or Y? What was the key to deciding it was the right product? Who were they buying it for? What questions did they have about familiar products or brands compared to unfamiliar ones?

Having a real shop taught the team how people felt, thought and acted when making purchase decisions. It also helped the constituents explain something abstract — purchase decisions — using a concrete, recent example — shopping at the Mock Shop.

Facilitator Notes

Time:
20-40 mins.

Difficulty:
★☆☆☆☆

Step 1: Have the team practice by partnering in groups of two. At least one person (Person A) in each team should have a mobile phone with them.

Step 2: Ask Person A to simply explain to their partner (Person B) how they enter a new contact into the phone.

Step 3: Have Person B use the Show Me technique with Person A.

Step 4: Have Person B use the Five Whys technique with Person A.

Step 5: Ask the team to come back together and ask, "What kind of information did you get from using Five Whys?" Then ask, "What kind of information did you get from using Show Me?"

METHOD: INTERVIEW TECHNIQUES

Through telling stories, human beings reveal important issues and opportunities in their daily experiences. Often, what people say they do and what they actually do are not the same thing. So it's important not just to rely on asking straight forward questions in an interview. Here are a few techniques for collecting rich stories in an interview.

TRY

Begin with a simple example, like how someone uses a mobile phone. Partner up and ask your partner to begin with a SHOW ME of how they entered the last contact into their address book. Next move on to the FIVE WHYS technique with your partner. Ask them to tell you about the last contact they entered into their address book and then five consecutive Why? questions.

DISCUSS

Compare and contrast the type of information you get from the different techniques. Let this inform your questioning techniques in the field.

SHOW ME

If you are in the interviewee's environment, ask him/her to show you the things they interact with (objects, spaces, tools, etc). Capture pictures and notes to jog your memory later. Or have them walk you through the process.

DRAW IT

Ask participants to visualize their experience through drawings and diagrams. This can be a good way to debunk assumptions and reveal how people conceive of and order their activities.

5 WHY'S

Ask "Why?" questions in response to five consecutive answers. This forces people to examine and express the underlying reasons for their behavior and attitudes.

THINK ALOUD

As they perform a process or execute a specific task, ask participants to describe aloud what they are thinking. This helps uncover users' motivations, concerns, perceptions, and reasoning.

DEVELOP YOUR MINDSET

Facilitator Notes

Time:
20-40 mins.

Difficulty:
★★★★★

Step 1: Ask the design team to look at the photo and identify what stands out to them. Note when people explain behaviors based on personal assumptions (i.e. "The man in the white lab coat seems to be the manager").

Step 2: Ask what past experience led to this explanation.

Step 3: Use 'opposite logic' to question the assumption the person has made (i.e. "Wouldn't those wearing lab coats need to be most sterile and therefore working closest with the machinery, not supervising?)

Step 4: Ask how the interpretation would change if a new piece of information were introduced (i.e. "What if I were to tell you that in this place white is the color that servants wear? How would you view this scene differently?").

Step 5: Ask the design team what they have learned from this exercise.

Step 6: Stress the importance of going into research with a "Beginner's Mind" and asking questions that you think you might already know the answers to, because you may be surprised by the answers.

The exercises listed under this step are valuable to put you in the right frame of mind for research. It is often difficult, but very important, for experts
and professionals to put aside what they know when they conduct research. Keeping an open mind takes practice. The three exercises here can provide you with this practice before you go into the field:

» Beginner's Mind
» Observe vs. Interpret

MINDSET: BEGINNER'S MIND

Beginner's Mind is critical when entering a familiar environment without carrying assumptions with you that are based on prior experience. This is often very hard to do since we interpret the world based on our experience and what we think we know. This lens of personal experience can influence what we focus on and can make us unable to see important issues.

WATCH OUT

Remind yourself frequently of the need to approach your Design Challenge with Beginner's Mind, especially when you are in the field conducting research.

TRY

Here is one exercise to learn how to see the world through the eyes of a Beginner. Look at the photo on the opposite page and answer the following questions:

» What stands out to you? What is happening?

» What personal experience did you draw on when you looked at the picture?

» How could you look at the photo as a Beginner, without making assumptions about what is happening?

» What questions would you ask if you knew nothing about the context or activity of the people in the photo?

MINDSET: OBSERVE VS. INTERPRET

Building empathy for the people you serve means understanding their behavior and what motivates them. Understanding behavior enables us to identify physical, cognitive, social and/or cultural needs that we can meet through the products, services and experiences we create. This exercise helps us differentiate between observation and interpretation of what we see, revealing our biases and lenses through which we view the world.

Facilitator Notes

Time:
20-40 mins.

Difficulty:
★★☆☆☆

Step 1: Ask the team "What do you see happening in this image?" Listen for responses that have built-in interpretations and remind people to describe only what they see at this point.

Step 2: Ask "What might be the reason for this behavior?" and have the team generate at least five different interpretations about why this might be happening.

If people are stuck, throw out an idea like : "This person is displaying her clothes to her neighbors as a sign of wealth by hanging them in a public space."

Step 3: Ask "What questions would you ask to find out the real answer?" and make a list of the questions that would help your team discover the right interpretation for an observation.

TRY

Use the photo on the opposite page to practice making the distinction between observations and interpretations.

WHAT DO YOU SEE HAPPENING IN THIS IMAGE?
Describe only what you see, don't interpret yet.

WHAT IS THE REASON FOR THIS BEHAVIOR?
List five different possible interpretations that might explain this person's behavior.

HOW WOULD YOU FIND OUT THE REAL ANSWER?
List five questions you could ask her to determine which interpretation is correct.

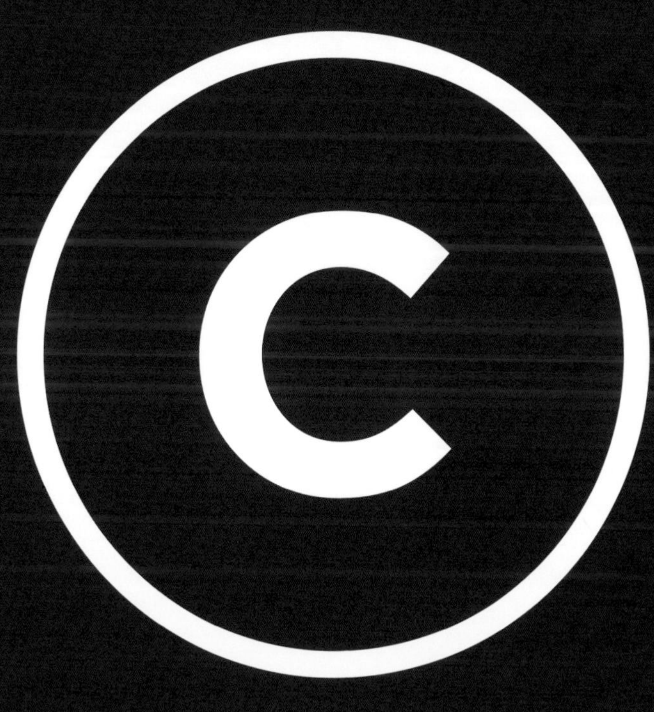

CREATE

INCREASING FARMER INCOME, CAMBODIA

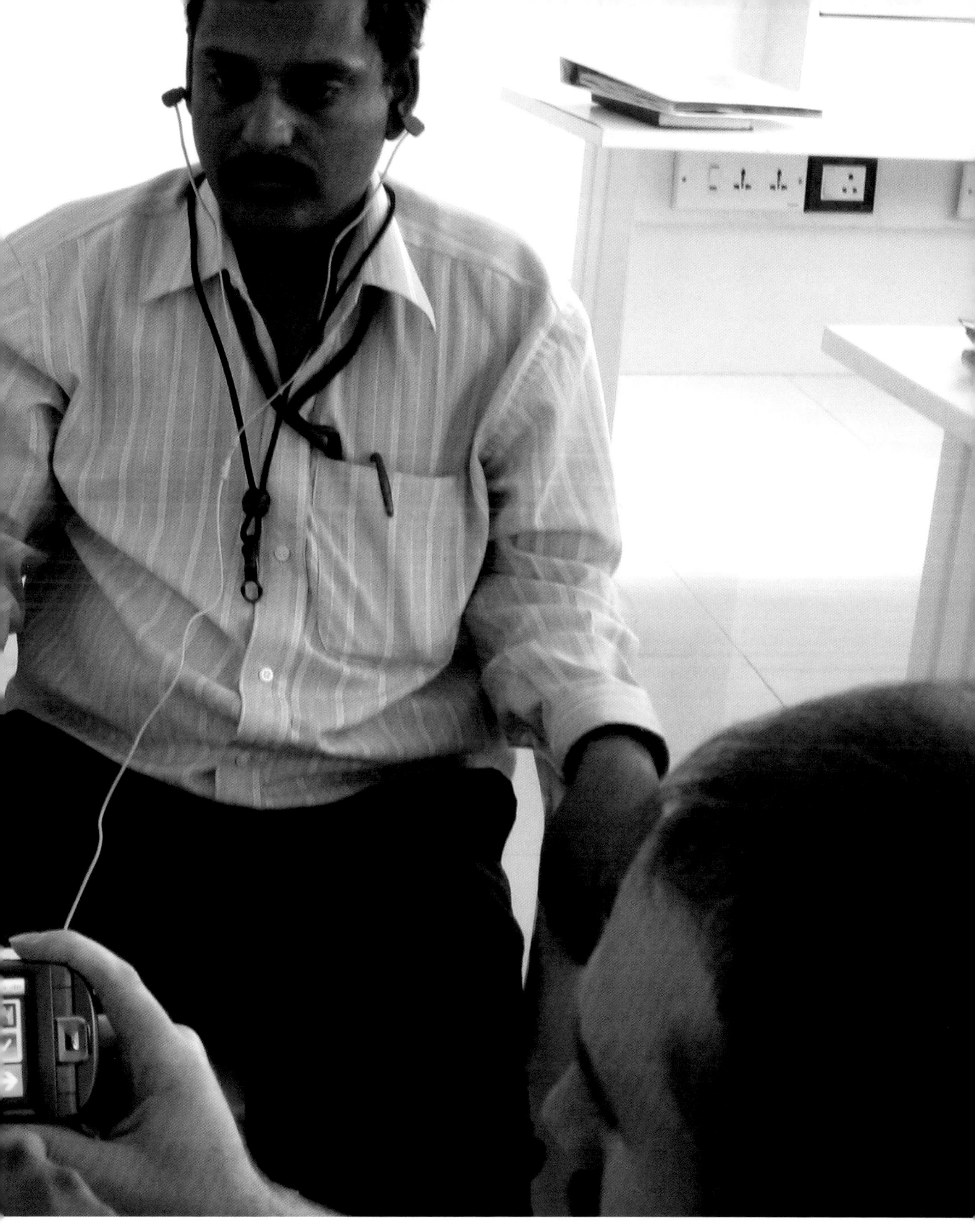

APPROPRIATE HEARING AID PROTOCOLS, INDIA

Taste

WATER STORAGE AND TRANSPORTATION, INDIA

CREATE: GOALS

To move from research to real-world solutions, you will go through a process of synthesis and interpretation. This requires a mode of narrowing and culling information and translating insights about the reality of today into a set of opportunities for the future. This is the most abstract part of the process, when the concrete needs of individuals are transformed into high-level insights about the larger population and system frameworks that the team creates.

With defined opportunities, the team will shift into a generative mindset to brainstorm hundreds of solutions and rapidly make a few of them tangible through prototyping. During this phase, solutions are created with only the customer Desirability filter in mind.

Goals of the Create Phase are:

» MAKING SENSE OF DATA
» IDENTIFYING PATTERNS
» DEFINING OPPORTUNITIES
» CREATING SOLUTIONS

“”

A new way to go beyond analysis, a way to create new solutions based on the voice of the customer.

—IDE VIETNAM

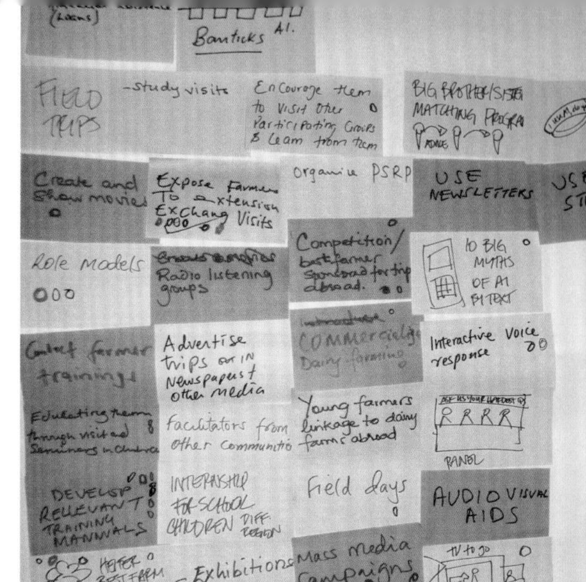

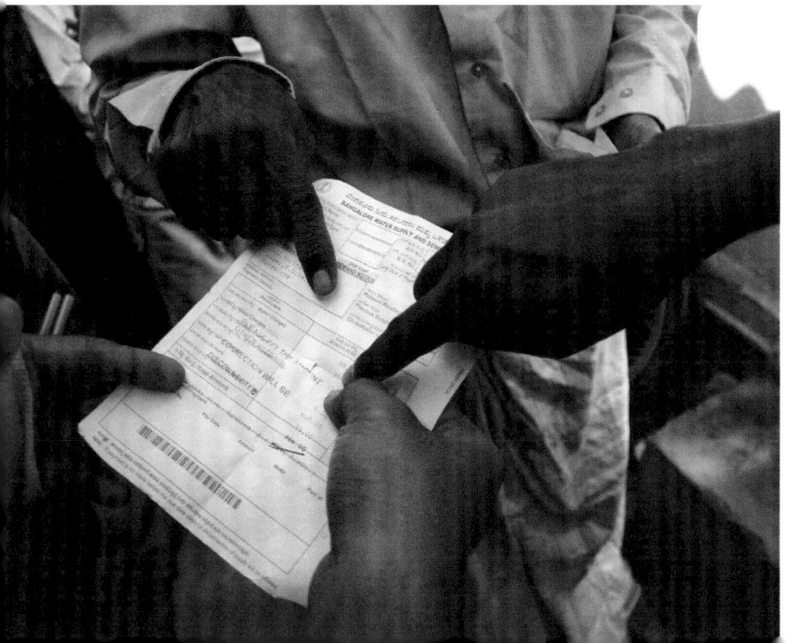

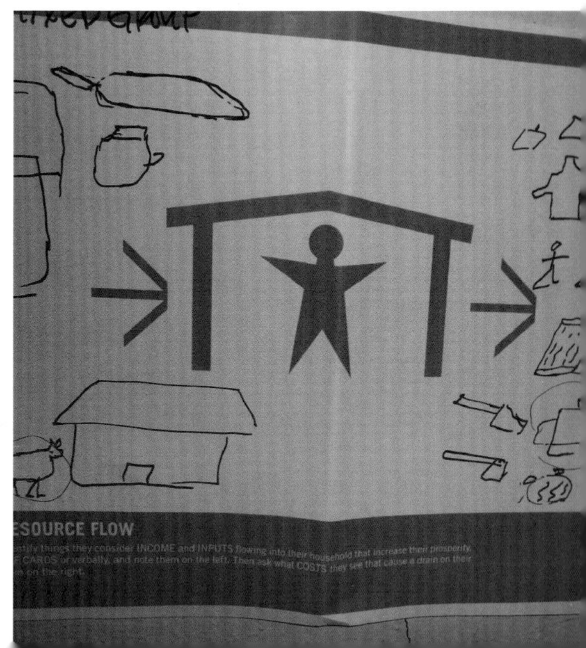

CREATE: OUTPUTS

Using both left-brain (logical) thinking and right-brain (creative) thinking, this phase will translate your research into a set of strategic directions and tangible solutions.

At the end of the Create phase, the team will have generated the following:

» OPPORTUNITIES
» SOLUTIONS
» PROTOTYPES

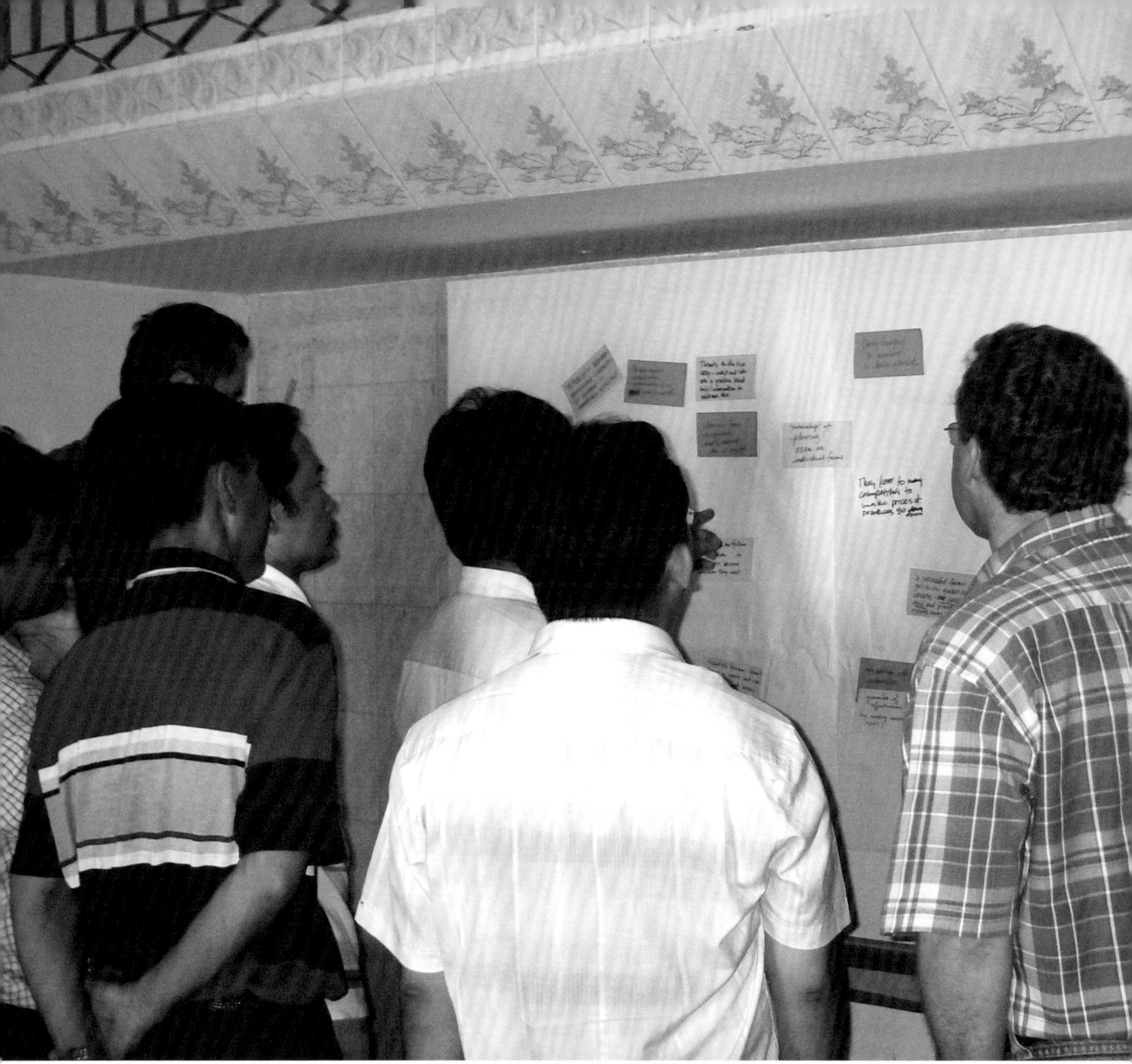

There are four key activities in the Create phase: synthesis, brainstorming, prototyping, and feedback.

CREATE: THEORY

Synthesis is the act of making sense of what we've seen and heard during the observations.

Synthesis takes us from inspiration to ideas, from stories to strategic directions.

By aggregating, editing and condensing what we've learned, synthesis enables us to establish a new perspective and identify opportunities for innovation.

Brainstorming with rules like Defer Judgment and Build on the Ideas of Others is a proven method for coming up with unexpected innovations.

Brainstorming makes us think expansively and without constraints.

The practice of generating truly impractical solutions often sparks ideas that are relevant and reasonable. It may require generating 100 ideas (many of which are mediocre) in order to come up with three truly inspirational solutions.

Prototyping is a methodology for making solutions tangible in a rapid and low-investment way. It's a proven technique for quickly learning how to design an offering right and for accelerating the process of rolling out solutions to the world.

Prototyping is about building to think, acknowledging that the process of making ideas real and tangible helps us to refine and iterate the ideas very quickly.

Creating many different prototypes that highlight different aspects of your product or service not only enables people to give honest feedback, but also prevents the team from getting attached to an idea prematurely.

Feedback is critical to the design process. It brings the constituents directly back into the design process.

Feedback inspires further iterations to make solutions more compelling for constituents.

DEVELOP THE APPROACH

Creation is about developing deeper understanding and translating that understanding into new innovations. There are many ways to do this, but the two most common are participatory approaches and empathic approaches. Use one or both of these approaches, develop your own, or draw upon different techniques when appropriate.

Facilitator Notes

Time:
Days-Weeks.

Difficulty:
★★★☆☆

Step 1. Identify constituents who would be good design team members. The criteria will vary from place to place and from challenge to challenge. For example, do you need people who are successful, respected, and/or politically powerful? Or would it be more valuable to have people who are typical community members? Or perhaps a mix of the two.

Step 2. Schedule a co-design session or series of sessions that works for everyone, and explain the process and goals of the session in advance.

Step 3. Conduct co-design sessions with attentions to the needs, goals, and priorities of the community.

METHOD: PARTICIPATORY CO-DESIGN

Having the team co-design solutions with people from the community and local value chain actors can be a great way to leverage local knowledge. It can also lead to innovations that may be better adapted to the context and be more likely to be adopted, since local people have invested resources in their creation.

Consider using participatory co-design when:

» you need a lot of local expertise and knowledge

» solutions from the "outside" will not be easily adopted

» the politics of a community require it

TRY #1

Facilitate a co-design workshop. Bring 8-20 people from the community together to design solutions to a challenge. Introduce the challenge by telling a few stories of problems that led to the design challenge. Then generalize those stories to How Might We? statements. Ask people to add their own stories or How Might We? questions. Brainstorm solutions with the participants and make sure you have the appropriate materials on hand to prototype.

TRY #2

Co-design over a longer period of time through an in-context immersion. By living with a family over a few days or weeks, you will have the opportunity to ask people to informally identify problems and work together with them in their home, farm, or community. This approach is also very good for spotting new problems and developing solutions to those problems in the moment they happen.

TRY #3

Find local experts and best practices. Ask different community members about the people who are considered to be successful. Schedule time with these people and leverage their knowledge to develop solutions together with them.

GENDER

Make sure to include women in the design team and female community members in the co-design. If living with a family, spend time equally with the husband, wife, extended family, and even the children. When hosting a co-design session, think about whether to have mixed-gender groups, or to have separate groups of men and women. When looking for local experts and best practices, ask who is considered an expert of both men and women, as well as less powerful groups.

CASE STUDY

ENGAGING LOCAL ARTISANS AS CO-DESIGNERS

An NGO and designer Kara Pecknold partnered with local weavers to help them market their woven products more widely and increase their economic power. Because the local artisans are the experts, this designer engaged these weavers as co-designers. The designer asked the weavers to draw a picture of what makes their weaving process or products unique as a way to understand how to differentiate their work.

Some drawings featured the plant that provides these weavers with their raw materials. They use the leaves from an invasive plant that is harming the environment of the Great Lakes Region of Africa. These weavers are turning an environmental problem into an economic opportunity. Based on these drawings and discussions, they identified the material they used as a key differentiator, and designed a logo for the weavers based on drawings of the plant.

Asking people to participate in the design process is helpful as a way to leverage local expertise. But it also can empower constituents to participate in their own destiny and helps balance the sometimes uneven power dynamic between the participant and the NGO team. In addition, engaging with participants in a visual way helped diminish problems created by language barriers.

COVAGA LOGO DESIGN PROCESS

INSIGHTS
& NEEDS
IDE

METHOD: EMPATHIC DESIGN

Creating solutions through empathy is a way for the design team to blend their expertise with the on-the-ground needs of people. Empathy means deep understanding of the problems and realities of the people you are designing for. It is important to do research across many different groups of people and to "walk in their shoes" before the Create phase if employing empathic design methods. By understanding people deeply, empathic design can lead to both appropriate and more breakthrough solutions. But this method challenges the design team to not just understand the problem mentally, but also to start creating solutions from a connection to deep thoughts and feelings.

Consider using empathic design when:

» the design team has specific skills required to develop solutions

» the solutions you are seeking are "new to the world"

» community politics make it difficult to select a few individuals to work with

GENDER

Include men and women in the design team to ensure a balance of perspectives.

TRY

When possible, recruit members of the community with the skills needed to be members of the design team.

WATCH OUT

Empathic design is not a method in which preconceived ideas and assumptions are substituted for grounded research and connection with end users. Although solutions are generated by the design team, the goal is to always have the people you are designing for in mind.

Facilitator Notes

Time:
Days-Weeks

Difficulty:
★★★☆☆

Step 1. Encourage the team to connect at both the rational and emotional levels with constituents.

Step 2. If team members start to judge or exoticize the behaviors or decisions of constituents, remind them that their task is to understand and empathize with people, not to judge them.

Step 3. Make sure the team has spoken with enough people in the Hear phase to develop empathy. If the design team still doesn't understand and feel the reasons for the behavior of constituents, go back to the field and conduct more research.

20/100
20/40
20/20
VisionSpring

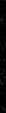

CASE STUDY

BRINGING EYECARE TO CHILDREN IN INDIAN VILLAGES

VisionSpring embarked on a project to shift its offer from selling reading glasses to adults in the developing world to providing comprehensive eye care to children.

In an initial brainstorm with the VisionSpring team after conducting field research, ideas centered around the notion that kids liked experiences designed for kids. The VisionSpring team met with experts, including pediatric eye doctors, and saw that the norm was to decorate spaces with stuffed animals and toys as a way to make kids feel comfortable.

During the prototyping process, the design team developed a number of prototypes for the eye screening process for kids. They went to the field armed with a number of prototypes to try and iterate on. Using the traditional eye chart, the Vision Entrepreneur and then the teacher administered the eye test. This was very intimidating to the kids and several burst into tears. To make it more approachable and less intimidating, the team also tried using a sillier eye-chart that had toys and animals on it. But it became too much like play, and chaos ensued.

The team took a step back and thought about what would be serious enough to keep the diagnostic session from becoming a raucous play session, but not so serious as to inspire tears.

Sitting in the schoolyard, the team reflected back on their own experiences as kids, recalled playing "house" and "doctor", where they would dress up with their friends and simulate adult behavior. Inspired by this role reversal/role play, the team thought: why not put the child in the position of authority? The team tried a protocol where the child would screen the eyes of the teacher, and then where they would screen each other. They had fun emulating adult behavior, and weren't intimidated by their peers.

Empathic design means thinking from the perspective of your users, and doing everything you can to feel and understand what they are experiencing. The team got in touch with what is fun and what is scary to kids in order to create an eye care experience that works for kids.

Facilitator Notes

Time:
4 Hours-Days

Difficulty:
★★☆☆☆

Step 1. Gather the design team together in a room with plenty of wall space. Optimally, the team should be sitting in a circle.

Step 2. Distribute post-it notes and markers. Have a flip chart or large sheets of paper nearby, as well as tape to attach these sheets to the wall.

Step 3. Tell the team to capture their notes, observations, and thoughts on the post-its as they speak. Everything that is said during story sharing should be captured in a note: life history, household details, income, aspirations, barriers, quotes, observations, etc.

Step 4. Ask each team member to share the story of the person(s) they met. Go through the stories one by one.

Step 5. Affix all the post-it notes to the flip chart or large pieces of paper on the wall. Use one large sheet per story. When the story is finished, hang it on the wall and move on to the next story. At the end of Story Sharing, you will have many sheets lined up on the wall with hundreds of post-it notes.

SHARE STORIES

Telling stories is about transforming the stories we heard during research into data and information that we can use to inspire opportunities, ideas and solutions. Stories are framed around real people and their lives, not summaries of information.

Stories are useful because they are accounts of specific events, not general statements. They provide us with concrete details that help us imagine solutions to particular problems.

TIP #1

It's best to share stories soon after research so that details are not lost. One team member should tell the story of the person(s) they met, while the rest of the team takes notes on post-its. Notes should be small pieces of information (no longer than a sentence) that will be easy to remember later. As a group you should be thinking, "What does this new information mean for the project?" Some tips on storytelling are below.

Be Specific
Talk about what actually happened. It helps to begin stories with "One time..." or "After such and such happened..."

Be Descriptive
Use your physical senses to give texture to your description.

Follow Reporting Rules
Cover the following topics: who, what, when, where, why, and how.

WATCH OUT

Try to avoid:

» Generalizing

» Prescribing (they should, would, could...)

» Hypothesizing

» Judging

» Evaluating or Assuming

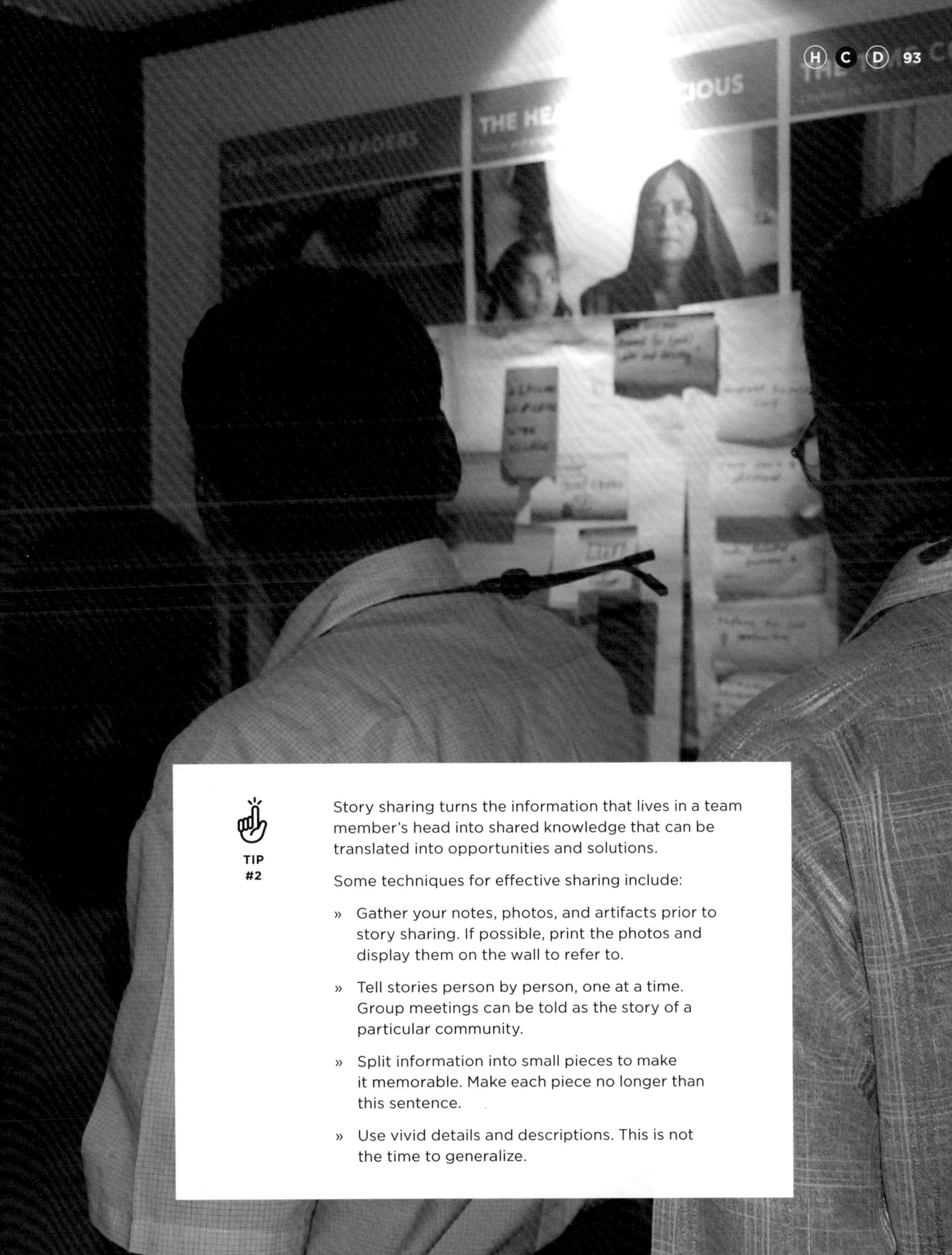

TIP #2

Story sharing turns the information that lives in a team member's head into shared knowledge that can be translated into opportunities and solutions.

Some techniques for effective sharing include:

» Gather your notes, photos, and artifacts prior to story sharing. If possible, print the photos and display them on the wall to refer to.

» Tell stories person by person, one at a time. Group meetings can be told as the story of a particular community.

» Split information into small pieces to make it memorable. Make each piece no longer than this sentence.

» Use vivid details and descriptions. This is not the time to generalize.

IDENTIFY PATTERNS

Making sense of your research is accomplished by seeing the patterns, themes, and larger relationships between the information. This process can be messy and difficult at times, but ultimately very rewarding. Seeing the patterns and connections between the data will lead you quickly toward real-world solutions. There are several steps listed here to take you through the process for you use selectively based on the subject matter.

» Extract Key Insights
» Find Themes
» Create Frameworks

METHOD: EXTRACT KEY INSIGHTS

Uncovering insights is about bringing visibility and clarity to previously hidden meaning.

WHAT IS AN INSIGHT?

» Insights are revelations – the unexpected things that make you sit up and pay attention.

» Insights extrapolate individual stories into overarching truths.

» Insights allow us to see our design challenge in a new light.

For example, a combination of an observation and quote from an interview yielded the following sample insight:

Observation: Farmers rely on farming information from their friends and neighbors, though they know this knowledge is limited.

Quote: "If the Privatized Extension Agent lived outside my area, I would want to visit his farm so I could see his production."

Insight: Trust-building and knowledge sharing happens through 'seeing is believing.'

Facilitator Notes

Time:
45-60 mins.

Difficulty:
★★★☆☆

Step 1. Ask the team to go to the wall with all the stories and choose 5 key post-its (stories, quotes, observations) that are most surprising, interesting, or provocative.

Step 2. Group these into related thoughts.

Step 3. Write a succinct Insight statement on a new post-it for each grouping that summarizes the big takeaway.

Step 4. Post these Insight post-its where all can see.

TIP #1

Select key information
Look across the information in the stories. Edit out the details that are not important – this is the time to let go of some of the detail. Choose the information that you find surprising, interesting, or worth pursuing.

TIP #2

Aggregate big thoughts
Are some of the thoughts linked? If so, aggregate them. Take several related pieces of information and re-write them as one big Insight.

TIP #3

Work at the same level
Check that the insights sit at the same level — that they are all big thoughts. If you find you have some lower level insights, consider whether they might be reframed at a higher level. If they need to be dropped a level, they may be best talked about as customer needs that inform and support the Insight.

CASE STUDY

FINDING INSIGHTS FOR EFFECTIVE MARKETING TO FARMERS

In Ethiopia, the IDE team looked over the information from the Story Sharing exercise and extracted over 20 key insights. About half of these came directly from the post-its that were written in Story Sharing, and the other half were written based on the information the team heard during Story Sharing.

Some of the insights the team identified were:

» School is a key channel for distributing information

» There is a strong need for an alternative to borrowing oxen

» Buying on credit is the default

» Mass media sells water pumps

Facilitator Notes

Time:
30-60 mins.

Difficulty:
★☆☆☆☆

Step 1. Have the team go to the wall or board where they have placed their key story and insight post-its and select the 5 most interesting quotes, observations and/or insights.

Step 2. On a new board, sort these into themes.

Step 3. Check to make sure the themes are at the same level. If a theme is too specific, prompt the team to find the bigger idea. If a theme is too broad or has too many different ideas under it, ask them to break it down into several buckets.

Step 4. When finished sorting, give each theme a title on a new post-it. Make sure there is enough space between or below the different theme categories to facilitate the next step of opportunity identification.

STEP 3

METHOD: FIND THEMES

Finding themes is about exploring the commonalities, differences, and relationships between the information.

Some ways to do this include:

Look for categories and buckets
Sort your findings into categories or buckets. Which ideas are related? Cluster together the findings that belong together into themes.

Consider the relationship between categories
Look for patterns and tensions in the way your themes relate to each other. Are they on the same level? Or are they talking about different kinds of things?

Group and re-group
Slice and dice the data in different ways to find meaning. Try moving the post-its around to form new groups.

Get input from the team
Explain the early buckets and themes to a broader group. Learn from their input and try alternative groupings.

TRY

Try the P.O.I.N.T. technique
Translate the Problems and Needs identified in storytelling into Insights (see previous Method) and Themes.

P = Problems
O = Obstacles
I = Insights
N = Needs
T = Themes

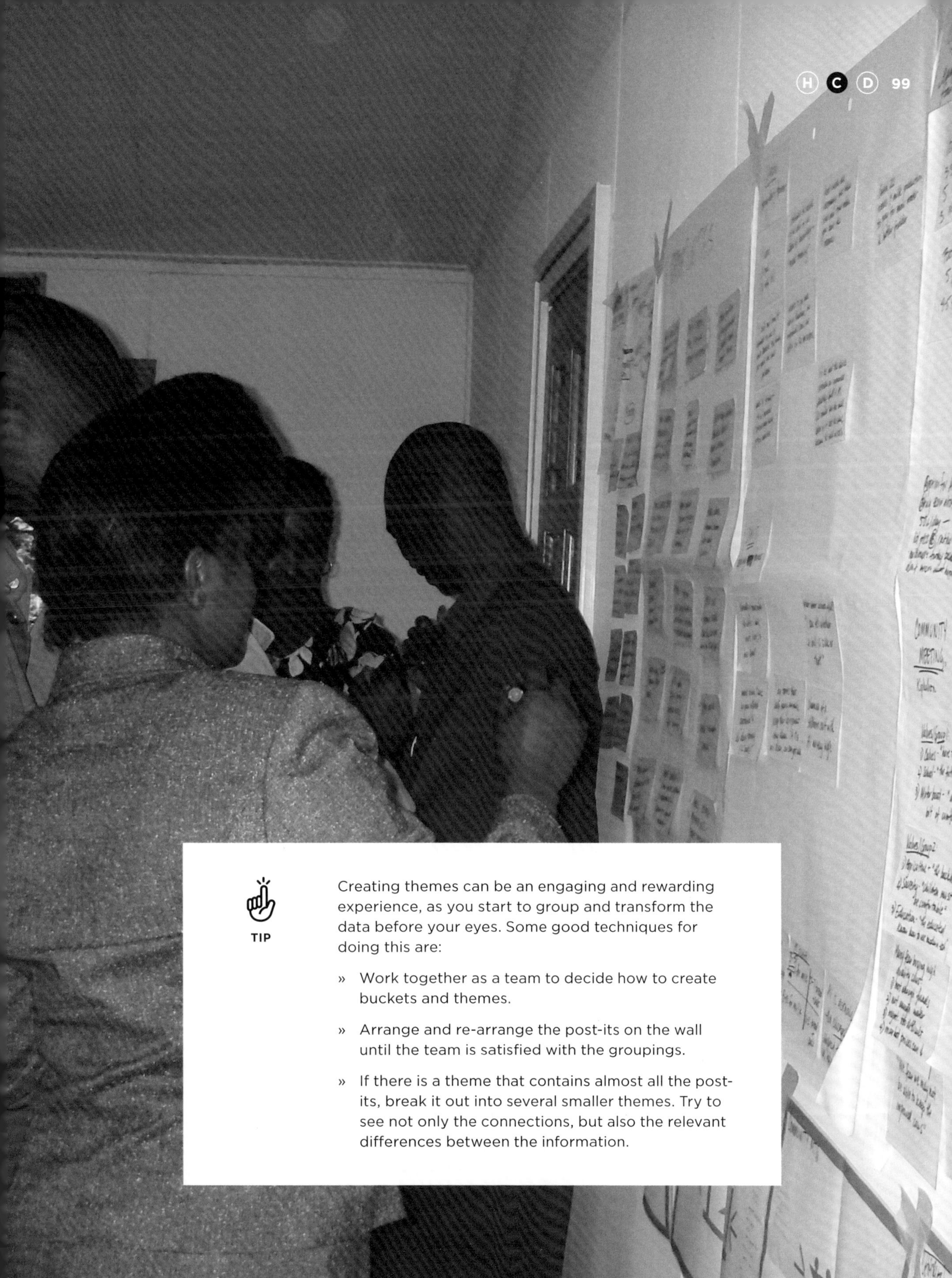

TIP

Creating themes can be an engaging and rewarding experience, as you start to group and transform the data before your eyes. Some good techniques for doing this are:

» Work together as a team to decide how to create buckets and themes.

» Arrange and re-arrange the post-its on the wall until the team is satisfied with the groupings.

» If there is a theme that contains almost all the post-its, break it out into several smaller themes. Try to see not only the connections, but also the relevant differences between the information.

METHOD: CREATE FRAMEWORKS

STEP 3

Frameworks allow you to begin putting the specific information from stories into a larger system context.

What is a framework?
A framework is a visual representation of a system. It shows the different elements or actors at play and highlights the relationships between them.

Using your framework
A good framework will help you see the issues and relationships in a clearer and more holistic way. Discuss what the framework implies for constituents, for other actors in the community, and for your organization. Use the framework to develop or build upon key insights. Capture those insights and add them to your growing list.

Facilitator Notes

Time:
1-2 Hours

Difficulty:
★★★★★

Not all design challenges will yield or require frameworks. If the team does not feel that this step is required for your challenge, skip it.

Step 1. Listen for moments in story sharing when the topic fits into a larger system or is linked to another piece of information.

Step 2. When team members start to suggest larger systemic structures or relationships between things, ask them if they can draw what they are saying. Consider the example framework types described here.

Step 3. Allow some time for your team to play with re-drawing their framework several times until they feel it represents what they want to say in a robust way.

GENDER

In many cases, it will make sense to create two different frameworks: one from the perspective of women in the community and one from the male perspective. To understand whether you need to dedicate attention to the different needs of women and men, ask yourself these questions:

» How do women's stories differ from those of men?

» Is gender itself a theme?

» Do women's stories tell a different story about household activities, income opportunities and barriers, and market relations than the stories obtained from men?

If you answered yes to these questions, think about creating two different frameworks that will yield different sets of opportunity areas for women and men.

TIP

If you are having trouble visualizing your own frameworks, here are some common types of frameworks that recur again and again.

Venn Diagram

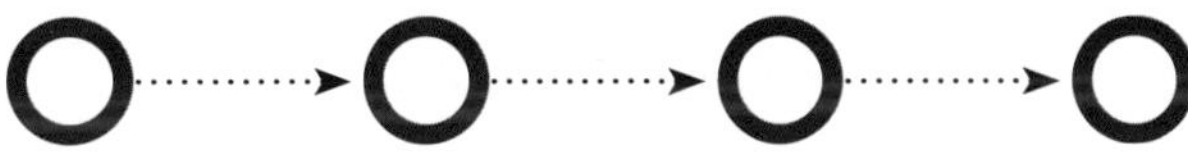

Process Map

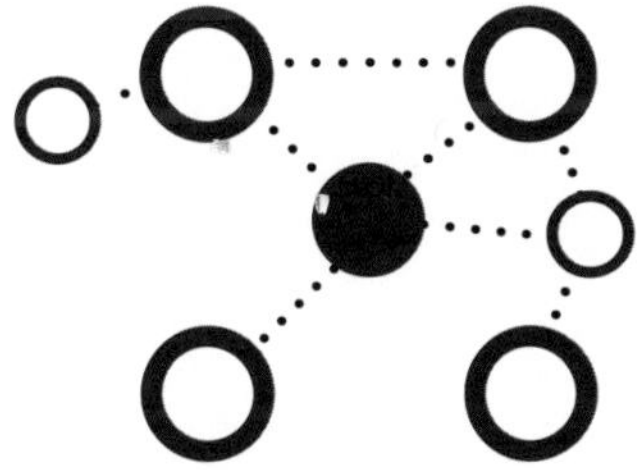

Relational Map

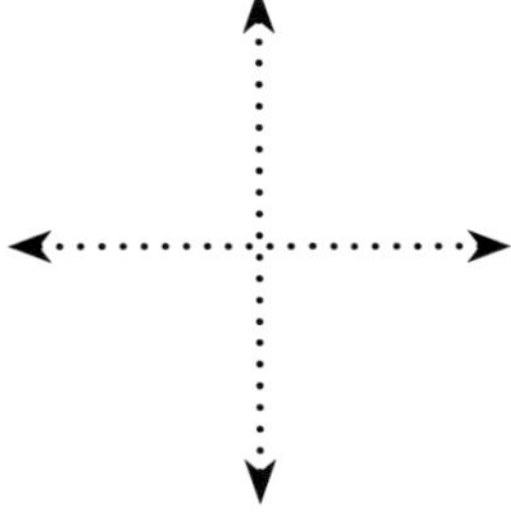

Two-by-Two Matrix

CREATE OPPORTUNITY AREAS

Once you have pulled out the themes and patterns from what you heard, you can start creating opportunity areas. The process of translating insights into opportunities is about moving from the current state to envisioning future possibilities. Opportunities are the springboard for ideas and solutions.

WHAT IS AN OPPORTUNITY AREA?

» An opportunity area is a stepping stone to idea generation.

» An opportunity is a rearticulation of problems or needs in a generative, future facing way.

» An opportunity area is not a solution. Rather, it suggests more than one solution. It allows the team to create many solutions.

FRAMING OPPORTUNITY AREAS

Opportunities start with the phrase "HOW MIGHT WE...?" to suggest a mindset of possibility.

TIP #1

Start each statement with "HOW MIGHT WE...?" and abbreviate on post-its to "HMW."

TIP #2

Use different color post-its for your opportunity statements than you used for insights. This will help to visually separate insights from opportunities for the next step.

Facilitator Notes

Time:
40 mins.-2 Hours

Difficulty:
★★★★☆

Step 1: Prepare your team to begin defining opportunity areas by telling them that this is where they will start to shift from analysis of information to creating new ideas.

Step 2: Distribute post-it notes and markers to everyone in the team. Ask the team to start their opportunities with the words "How Might We...?"

Step 3: Spend at least 15 minutes on each theme generating Opportunity Statements for that theme. Place the post-its next to the theme area.

Step 4: If the team gets stuck, read the insights from each theme area as a way to jolt the creativity of the team. For example, for each insight posted, ask the team to come up with at least one "How Might We..." statement.

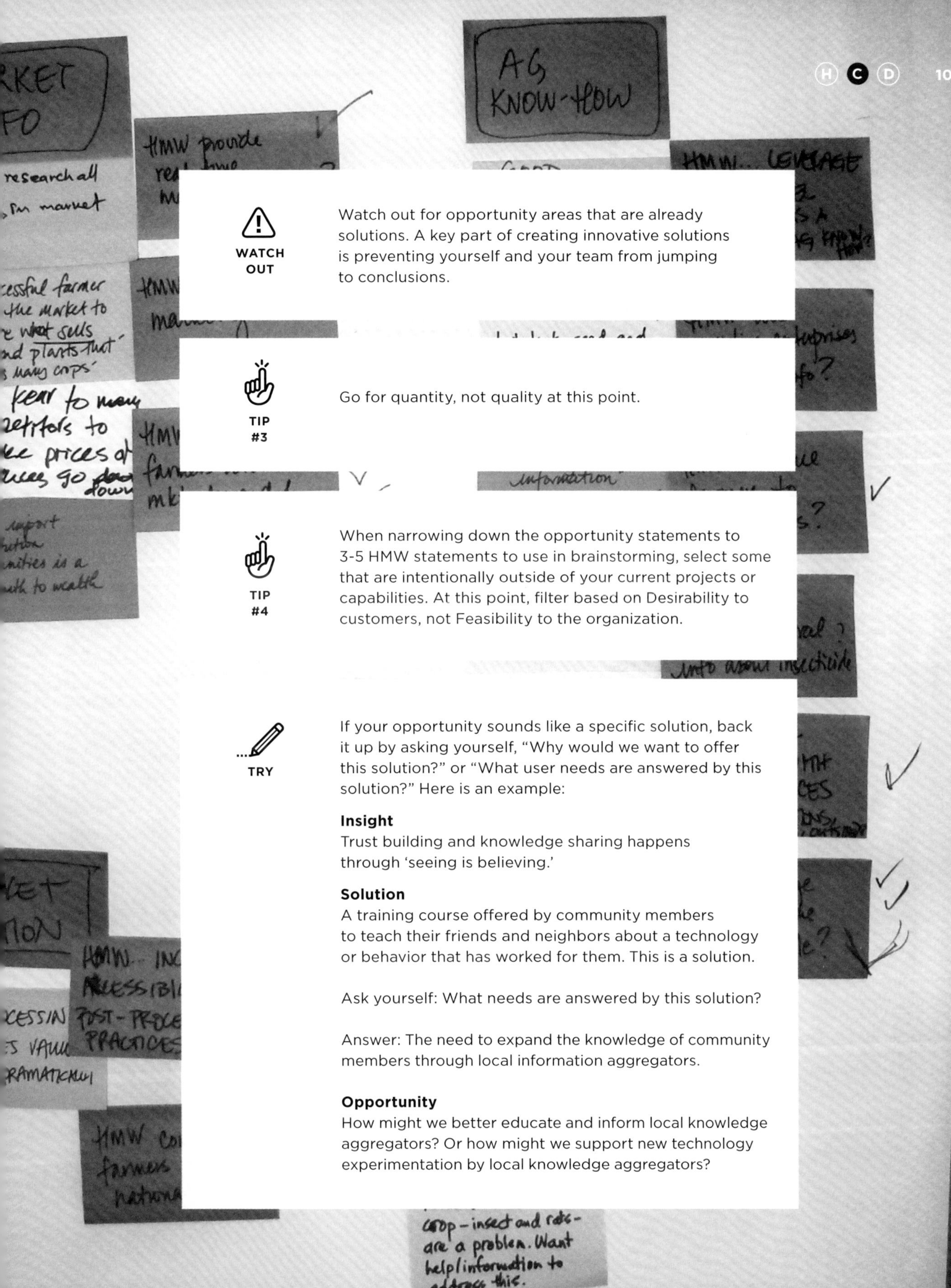

WATCH OUT

Watch out for opportunity areas that are already solutions. A key part of creating innovative solutions is preventing yourself and your team from jumping to conclusions.

TIP #3

Go for quantity, not quality at this point.

TIP #4

When narrowing down the opportunity statements to 3-5 HMW statements to use in brainstorming, select some that are intentionally outside of your current projects or capabilities. At this point, filter based on Desirability to customers, not Feasibility to the organization.

TRY

If your opportunity sounds like a specific solution, back it up by asking yourself, "Why would we want to offer this solution?" or "What user needs are answered by this solution?" Here is an example:

Insight
Trust building and knowledge sharing happens through 'seeing is believing.'

Solution
A training course offered by community members to teach their friends and neighbors about a technology or behavior that has worked for them. This is a solution.

Ask yourself: What needs are answered by this solution?

Answer: The need to expand the knowledge of community members through local information aggregators.

Opportunity
How might we better educate and inform local knowledge aggregators? Or how might we support new technology experimentation by local knowledge aggregators?

Facilitator Notes

Time:
45-60 mins.

Difficulty:
★★★★☆

Step 1. Prepare 3-5 "How Might We...?" opportunity statements from those generated previously. Place each statement on a separate wall or board. Give each person post-it notes and a marker.

Step 2. Remind people of the rules of brainstorming. Tell them to be very specific about the ideas they are proposing. Use big markers (not pens) so everyone can see what the idea is. Write only one idea per post-it.

Step 3. Begin by asking the group to generate a list of barriers related to the opportunity statement.

Step 4. Protect all participants by enforcing the Rules of Brainstorming. If ideas slow down, prompt the group to think about one of the barriers listed during the warm-up. Or share a story from the research to spark thinking (i.e. "So what ideas would encourage Shashu to adhere to her medication?")

Step 5. When the ideas really slow down, switch to a new opportunity area. This might be 15-30 minutes per HMW.

BRAINSTORM NEW SOLUTIONS

Brainstorming gives permission to think expansively and without any organizational, operational, or technological constraints.

Some people think of brainstorms as undisciplined conversation. But conducting a fruitful brainstorm involves a lot of discipline and a bit of preparation.

The practice of generating truly impractical solutions often sparks ideas that are relevant and reasonable. It may require generating 100 ideas (many of which are silly or impossible) in order to come up with those three truly inspirational solutions.

TIP

SEVEN BRAINSTORMING RULES

» **Defer judgment**
There are no bad ideas at this point. There will be plenty of time to judge ideas later.

» **Encourage wild ideas**
It's the wild ideas that often create real innovation. It is always easy to bring ideas down to earth later!

» **Build on the ideas of others**
Think in terms of 'and' instead of 'but.' If you dislike someone's idea, challenge yourself to build on it and make it better.

» **Stay focused on topic**
You will get better output if everyone is disciplined.

» **Be visual**
Try to engage the logical and the creative sides of the brain.

» **One conversation at a time**
Allow ideas to be heard and built upon.

» **Go for quantity**
Set a big goal for number of ideas and surpass it! Remember there is no need to make a lengthy case for your idea since no one is judging. Ideas should flow quickly.

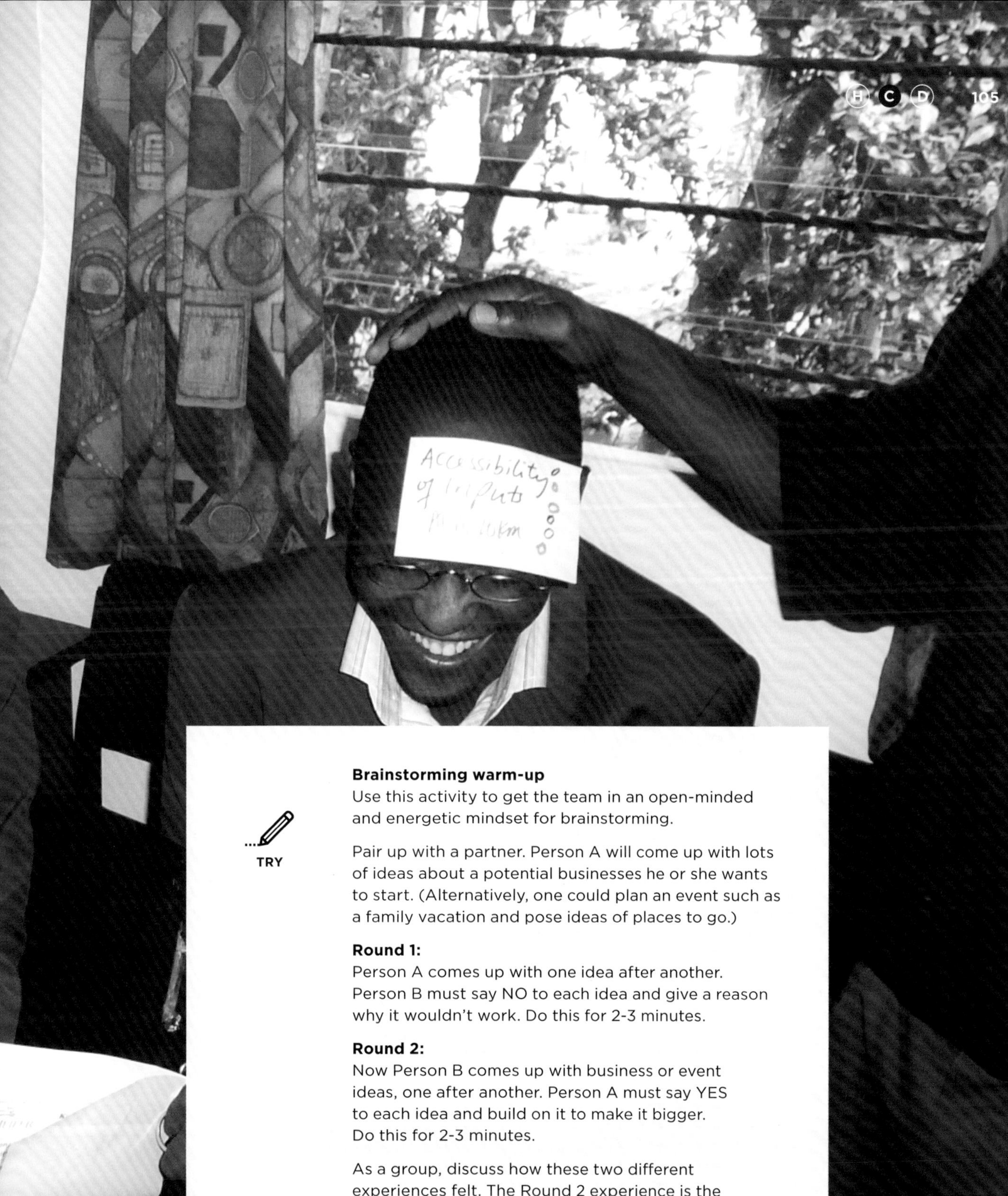

TRY

Brainstorming warm-up
Use this activity to get the team in an open-minded and energetic mindset for brainstorming.

Pair up with a partner. Person A will come up with lots of ideas about a potential businesses he or she wants to start. (Alternatively, one could plan an event such as a family vacation and pose ideas of places to go.)

Round 1:
Person A comes up with one idea after another. Person B must say NO to each idea and give a reason why it wouldn't work. Do this for 2-3 minutes.

Round 2:
Now Person B comes up with business or event ideas, one after another. Person A must say YES to each idea and build on it to make it bigger. Do this for 2-3 minutes.

As a group, discuss how these two different experiences felt. The Round 2 experience is the environment the team will want to create for a successful brainstorm.

Facilitator Notes

Time:
45-60 mins.

Difficulty:
★★★☆☆

Step 1. Ask teams to partner in teams of 2-4. Small teams help everyone to have a role.

Step 2. Ask teams to pick one solution from the brainstorming boards. You may choose to offer a range of criteria: two teams working on solutions they're "most passionate about," one group on "most feasible " and one on "furthest out" or "long term".

Step 3. Prompt teams to spend no more than 30-45 minutes making their chosen solution tangible, using one of the prototyping forms described here or creating new ones.

Step 4. Give each team 5 minutes to share their idea back with the larger group to get initial feedback. Encourage teams to include an enactment of the experience of use, even if they have a paper-based prototype. Prompt groups to identify what customer needs their prototype addresses and what key questions they still have.

MAKE IDEAS REAL

Prototyping is about building to think. This means creating the solution so that it can be communicated to others and making the idea better. Prototyping allows you to quickly and cheaply make ideas tangible so they can be tested and evaluated by others - before you've had time to fall in love with them.

What is prototyping?

» BUILD TO THINK: Prototypes are disposable tools used throughout the concept development process, both to validate ideas and to help generate more ideas. Prototypes are a powerful form of communication and force us to think in realistic terms about how someone would interact with the concept.

» ROUGH, RAPID, RIGHT: Prototypes are not precious. They should be built as quickly and cheaply as possible.

» ANSWERING QUESTIONS: It is essential to know what question a prototype is being used to answer, for example about desirability, usefulness, usability, viability, or feasibility.

Why prototype?

» To develop a deeper understanding of what an idea means and to reveal questions the team needs to answer.

» To create an internal dialogue about how the concept works and external communication about the concept.

Imagine the Value Proposition

For each prototype, answer these questions to start building the value of the idea:

» Who will benefit from this idea? What is the value to the end customers?

» Why and how is this idea better than alternative options?

» How much is this benefit worth to them?

» How much would they be willing to pay for this benefit"

» How might this payment be collected?

TIP

COMMON PROTOTYPE FORMS

Models:
A physical model of a product, shown above, makes a 2-dimensional idea come alive in 3 dimensions. Using rough materials allows you to quickly mock up low-fidelity prototypes.

Storyboards:
Imagining the complete user experience through a series of images or sketches.

Role-play:
The emotional experience with a product or service is sometimes best expressed by acting it out with team members taking on the role of the constituent or customer.

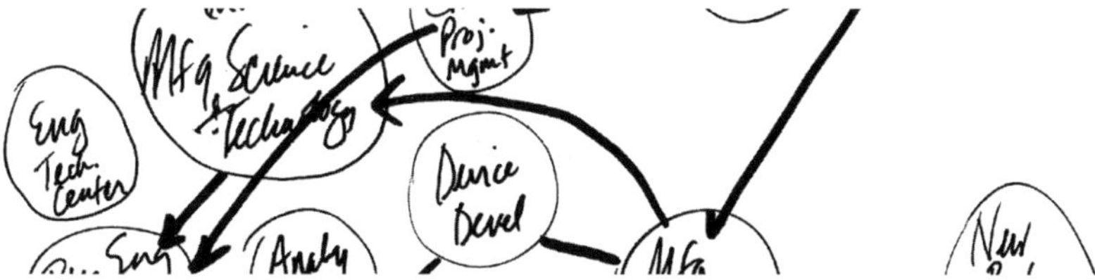

Diagrams:
Mapping is a great way to express a space, process, or structure. Consider how ideas relate to each other, and how the experience changes over time.

Facilitator Notes

Time:
1-1.5 Hours

Difficulty:
★★★☆☆

Step 1. Ask team members to prepare how to present their solutions to participants. It's not necessary to give behind-the-scenes organizational information to them.

Step 2. Have teams practice presenting solutions to the rest of the group—enactment is especially effective. Invite others to help simplify and clarify the presentation and identify focus questions to be answered in research.

Step 3. Ask teams to standardize a script about the solution so it is delivered consistently at each feedback session. Write down key questions to ask in follow-up.

Step 4. When introducing the feedback session to the customer group, explain you want honest feedback—even if negative—and that the team has spent minimal time prototyping.

GATHER FEEDBACK

After solutions have been generated, it's time to take them back out to participants to gather feedback.

WATCH OUT

Don't invest too much time perfecting the ideas before feedback – the point of re-engaging customers is to change the solutions, not to prove that they are perfect. The best feedback is that which makes you rethink and redesign.

How to solicit feedback
A great way to get honest feedback is to take several executions out to people. When there is only one concept available, people may be reluctant to criticize. However, when allowed to compare and contrast, people tend to speak more honestly.

Whose feedback to solicit
Speaking to new participants in a different region from where you did your research is a way to explore the generalizability of a solution. You may choose to speak to a mix of both new people and to those you have spoken with before.

Try to include all stakeholders who would touch the concept; in addition to the end user, include manufacturers, installers, service providers, distributors, retailers, etc.

What questions to pursue
For each prototype, identify 3-4 questions you'd like answer about desirability or use case during the feedback session.

Keep careful notes of the feedback, both positive and negative, and the new questions the team needs to answer about the solution.

TIP

The goal is to solicit honest feedback, even if it is negative. It's better to know early on before much investment has been made that a solution is not desirable. Here are a few tips in presenting yourselves and your solutions to participants:

Don't try to sell the idea.
Present solutions with a neutral tone, highlighting both pros and cons of a solution.

Vary group size.
Begin with a large group (10-15) to present the solution, then break into smaller groups, one per solution for a more intimate conversation.

Adapt on the fly.
If it becomes clear that there is one aspect of the solution that is distracting people from the core idea, feel free to eliminate this piece or change it.

Ask participants to build on the ideas.
If a participant asks a question like, "Can this service be purchase by the community or just an individual?" Ask the question back to them: "*Should* the service be purchased by the community or individual?" Another valuable question is, "How could this be better for you?" It invites the participant to help improve the idea or give additional critique.

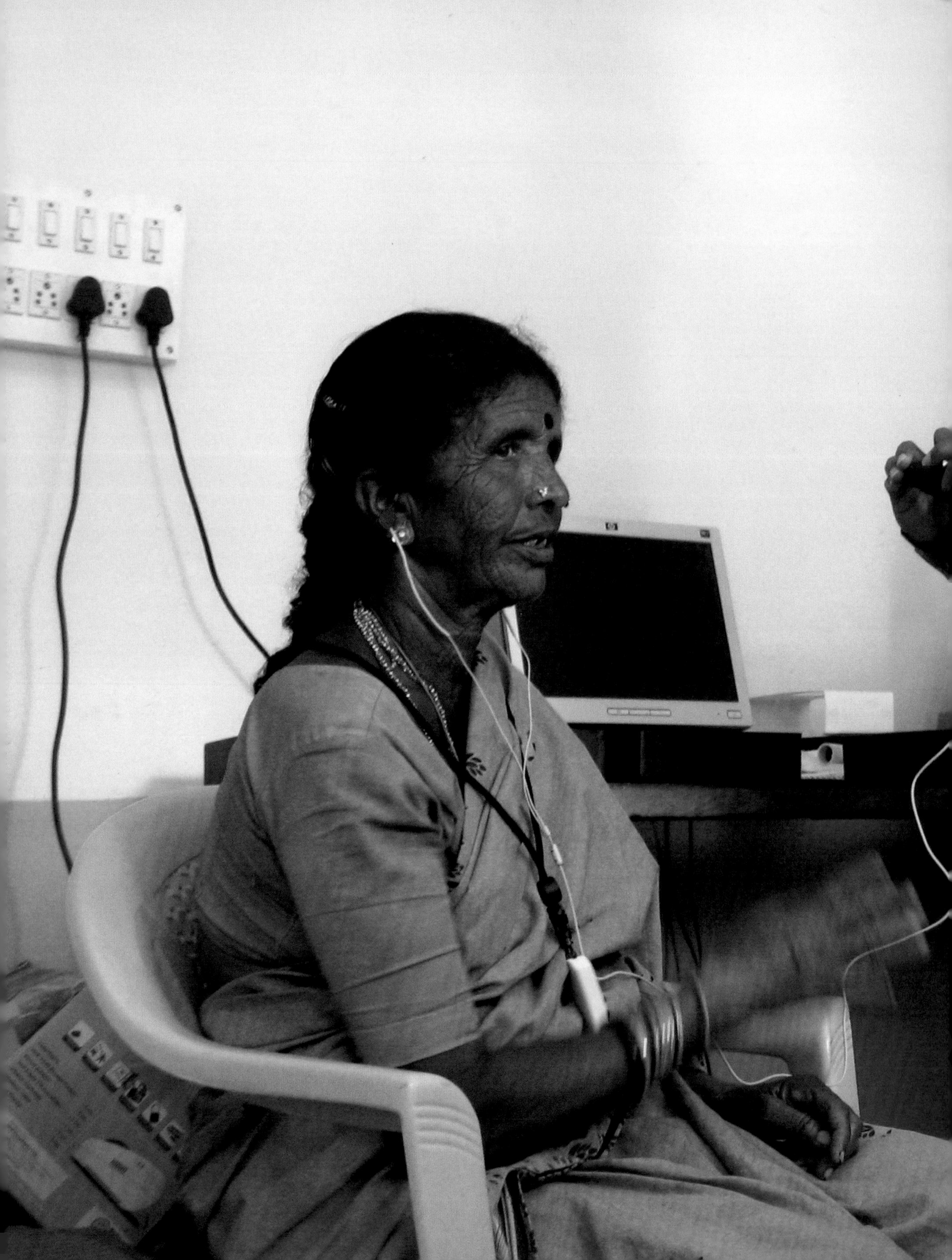

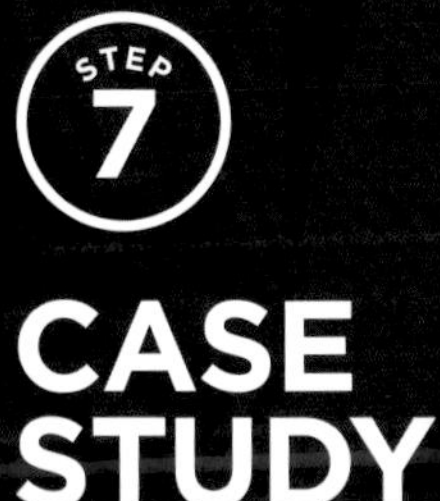

CASE STUDY

TESTING HEARING AID PROTOCOLS FOR RURAL INDIA

The design challenge for this IDEO project was to make hearing aids more accessible in rural India. One key hurdle was creating a diagnostic process that could be effectively administered outside a medical setting by minimally-trained local technicians.

During the initial research, the team learned about the constraints associated with fitting a hearing aid. They developed a process prototype that included a fitting protocol, a technician kit with tools for fitting a hearing aid, and technician training materials. The team started by training two local people as technicians in less than a day, and then went to villages to watch the newly trained technicians try the protocol with people who have trouble hearing.

While watching the technicians on the first day in a village, the team quickly saw that the protocol was too complex. It took too long to explain to potential customers how to complete the tests. The team immediately set to simplifying the protocol, and then trained a new pair of technicians on the newly simplified protocol. To the team's surprise, while the next village visit went more smoothly, there were still some challenges due to complexity. The team conducted a third round of simplification, and final testing confirmed that the protocol was finally simple enough and effective enough to work.

Gathering feedback early allows you to focus on how to improve your design and helps you identify problems in your designs that you may not notice in an artificial setting. As in this example, it is often possible to make changes and improvements to the design between feedback sessions, so that the team continues to learn and improve the solution.

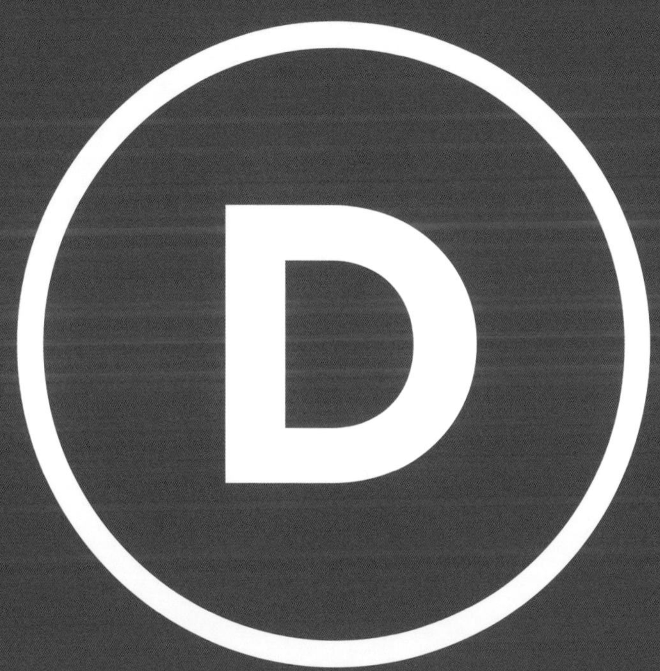

DELIVER

EYECARE FOR CHILDREN, INDIA

WATER STORAGE AND TRANSPORTATION, INDIA

INCREASING SMALLHOLDERS FARMER INCOME, ETHIOPIA

DELIVER: GOALS

Once the design team has created many desirable solutions, it is time to consider how to make these feasible and viable. The Deliver phase will move your top ideas toward implementation.

The activities offered here are meant to complement your organization's existing implementation processes and may prompt adaptations to the way solutions are typically rolled out.

In the Deliver Phase, your team will:

» IDENTIFY REQUIRED CAPABILITIES
» CREATE A MODEL FOR FINANCIAL SUSTAINABILITY
» DEVELOP AN INNOVATION PIPELINE
» PLAN PILOTS & MEASURE IMPACT

“”

Tools to catapult solutions to the next steps of implementation.

—IDE CAMBODIA

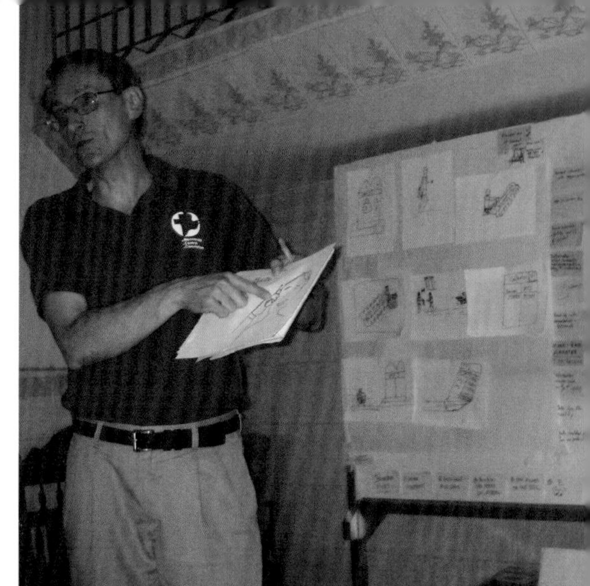

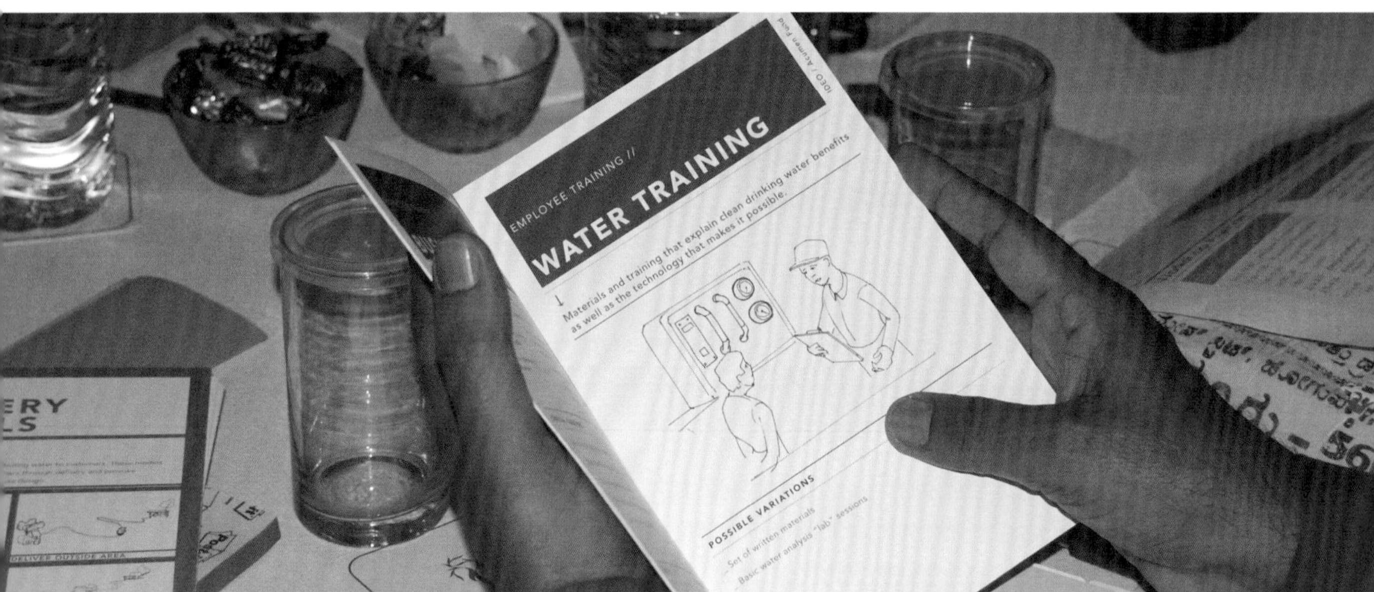

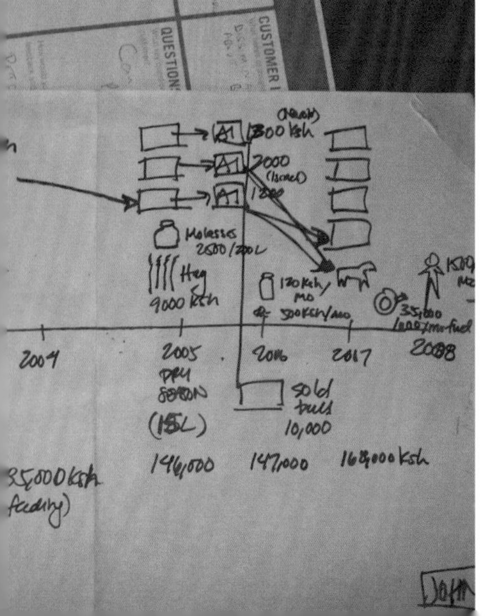

DELIVER: OUTPUTS

This phase will challenge the team to create the elements necessary to make the solution successful, and to track the impact of the solution.

In the Deliver phase, you will produce:

» **FEASIBILITY ASSESSMENT**
» **VIABILITY ASSESSMENT**
» **INNOVATION PIPELINE**
» **IMPLEMENTATION PLAN**
» **LEARNING PLAN**

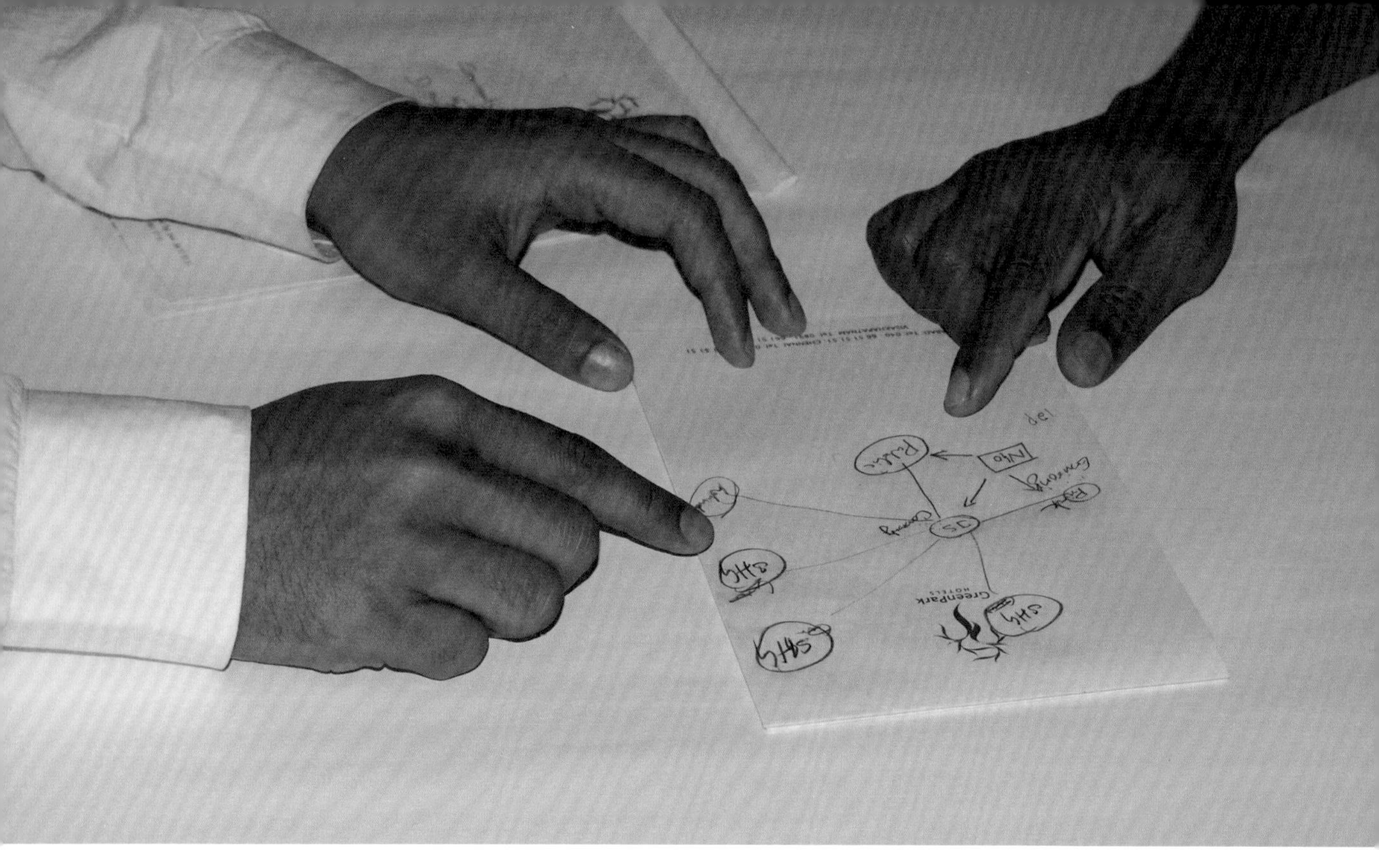

Delivering solutions to your consituents means you will need to build the capabilities and financial models that will ensure that the solutions are implemented well and can be sustained over the long term. You will also need to create a plan for on-going learning and iteration.

DELIVER: THEORY

Delivering solutions that are new to the world involves creating low-investment, low-cost ways of trying out your ideas in a real-world context.

The team can design a handful of mini-pilots that precede and inform the full pilot program. Mini-pilots might engage actors who are different from the group of stakeholders for the final implementation. For example, in a mini-pilot, the NGO or social enterprise might play certain roles that will ultimately be held by partners in order to gain a deeper understanding of how the system should work and to be more informed when soliciting and training partners.

Implementation is an iterative process that will likely require many prototypes, mini-pilots and pilots to perfect the solution and support system.

Piloting an idea before it goes to market not only allows you to understand the solution better, but also helps you identify what it will take for your organization to deliver that idea to the community.

Every organization is optimized to achieve what it currently does. If you want to achieve different outcomes, you often need to do things differently than you know and do right now—whether it is about finding new talent, developing new skills, building new external partnerships, or creating new processes.

The Human-Centered Design process doesn't limit the solution by the current constraints of the organization.

This process invites you to work in the belief that new things are possible, and that you can evolve both the solutions that you deliver and the way your organization is designed, simultaneously.

In addition, Human-Centered Design integrates design and measurement methods in a continuous learning cycle. By encouraging on-going measurement, evaluation, and iteration, the solutions developed stay grounded in real-world impact and continue to evolve.

Facilitator Notes

Time:
30-45 mins.

Difficulty:
★★★★★

Focus on one solution at a time and take the team through the following exercise. Alternatively, the larger team can be split into smaller teams of two or three, with each smaller team focusing on one solution.

Step 1: On a board or flip chart, write "Customer Value." Ask the team to identify how each solution will provide value to the end customer. Write everything down. Ask the team to answer the question: "How much is this worth to the end customer?" Write down the figure on the chart.

Step 2: On a separate board or flip chart, write "Revenue Sources." Ask the team to identify who will pay for the product or service. How much will each actor pay? How will the payments be received? Use the example fee models in the "Try" text box to help.

Continues next page.

DEVELOP A SUSTAINABLE REVENUE MODEL

The long-term success of solutions depends upon the intentional design of a revenue stream that can sustain the offering over time. Let the value provided to the end customer be your entry point as you design the support systems around the solution. For this Viability Assessment, answer the following questions for each solution.

TIP

1. Customer Value Proposition

» What is the value proposition for the end customer? Refer back to prototypes and customer feedback, highlighting the aspects customers found most important.

» How much is this worth to the end customer?

2. Revenue Sources

» Is the solution a product, a service or both?

» How much do customers pay?

» How do customers pay: in cash, in kind, in labor, in other?

3. Stakeholder Incentives

» How does this solution deliver value to each stakeholder involved?

» What are the stakeholders' incentives to participate? What are challenges or disincentives? How might we adapt the solution to avoid these disincentives?

TRY

Consider the following fee models to inspire your thinking. One exercise is for the design team to go down the list of models and ask:

"What would our solution look like if it were offered by: ...?"

» Membership/Subscription
» Gift it, share the income produced
» Give the product, sell the refill
» Subsidize
» Give the product, sell the service
» Service only
» Pay-per-use

Facilitator Notes
(Continued)

Step 3: On another board or flip chart, write "Stakeholder Incentives." Ask the team to identify all stakeholders or players in the value chain who will be affected by the solution. Go through each actor and ask: "What is this group's incentives to participate in or help this solution?" If there is a group that has a disincentive to participate in the solution, ask: "How might we adapt the solution to encourage their participation?"

Step 4: If the team has split into smaller teams, have the group come back together to share.

CASE STUDY

MODELING REVENUE FOR NEW SERVICES

For the Today's Market Prices solution, the IDE Cambodia team identified the desirability of payment-in-kind options through customer feedback:

Customer Value Proposition

» Connection to Privatized Extension Agent with real-time market pricing to inform where to sell large-quantity crops.
» Connection to traders who collect from farms and sell crops at selected markets.

Revenue Sources

» Payment in kind per use (price deducted from sales of crop at each collection)
» Mobile phone provided a no cost (through phone donation program)
» Free calls to designated number of Privatized Extension Agent

Stakeholder Incentives

» Privatized Extension Agent receives fee per information request
» Crop Collector expands his farmer clientele and receives a % from crops sold
» Mobile provider is paid for calls made to PEA numbers; expands potential customer base for calls/SMS sent outside the free number

IDENTIFY CAPABILITIES REQUIRED FOR DELIVERING SOLUTIONS

The capabilities of your organization and partners will help inform the feasibility of solutions. Begin by thinking about the experience of the end customer—where and how the community members or end-user will purchase or experience this solution. Then identify the range of capabilities required for making this real. A challenge for the design team is to identify many possible models for delivery that leverage different partners and channels.

TIP

To identify the capabilities required to make each solution feasible, answer the following questions for each solution:

1. Distribution

» Where, when, how, and why might the customer experience this solution?

» Which actors and channels will touch the solution?

» What other channels could be used to reach customers?

» What is the range of possible ways this solution could be delivered?

2. Capabilities Required

» What human, manufacturing, financial, and technological capabilities are required for creating and delivering this solution?

» Which of these capabilities do we have in our country location? Which do we have in our international location? And which capabilities will need to be found in partners?

» Would we need to grow any capabilities on this list?

3. Potential Partners

What organizations or individuals have capabilities that we do not? What is our relationship with them currently? How might we reach out to them and show the value of engaging with our organization on this solution?

Facilitator Notes

Time:
30-45 mins.

Difficulty:
★☆☆☆☆

Focus on one solution at a time and take the team through the following exercise. Alternatively, the larger team can be split into smaller teams of two or three, with each smaller team focusing on one solution.

Step 1: Write "Distribution" on a board or flip chart. Have the team identify all the possible actors who could deliver this solution. Write each actor on a post-it note. Ask the team to list the pros and cons of each of the different delivery possibilities.

Step 2: Write "Capabilities" on a separate board or flip chart. List the human, manufacturing, financial, and technical capabilities that will be required for each solution. Indicate if the capability exists in your local organization, if it exists somewhere else in your network, or whether you will have to partner.

Step 3: For the solutions that you will need to partner, create a list of potential partners. Narrow to a smaller set of partners. Ask the team to list the first step they would take to pursue the top partners identified.

Step 4: If you have split into smaller groups, ask the teams to come together to share their thoughts.

SOLUTION TODAY'S MARKET PRIC

CAPABILITY REQUIRED	L O
1. MARKET INFO COLLECTOR	
2. DATA AGGREGATION 	
3. INFO DISSEMINATION	
'IT' INFRASTRUCTURE	
5. FARMER CONNECTION	
6. PRICE MODELING	
7.	

DO: CAPABILITY ASSESSMENT

List the capabilities that will be required to realize this concept.
Place a plus (+) if this capability already exists in the local office, internatioinal c
Place a minus (-) if this capability will need to be developed in the local office
partners.

CASE STUDY

DELIVERING TODAY'S MARKET PRICES

In Cambodia, the IDE design team created a solution called "Today's Market Prices," real-time market crop price information to farmers. The team identified one model to deliver this to customers involving two key partners: Privatized Extension Agents and Crop Collectors.

Distribution

» Centralized information gathering & distribution
» Information distributed by Privatized Extension Agents (PEAs) upon request of the farmer
» Farmer requests info by mobile phone provided with free calls to PEA
» Crops & fee collected by Crop Collector

Capabilities Required

» Market price information collection daily (or multiple times a day)
» Market price information aggregation & distribution to Privatized Extension Agents
» Communication channels between farmers & PEAs via mobile phone
» Crop collection & sales
» Fee collection

Potential Partners

» Government market information sources
» Privatized Extension Agent
» Mobile phone donor program
» Mobile service provider
» Crop Collector

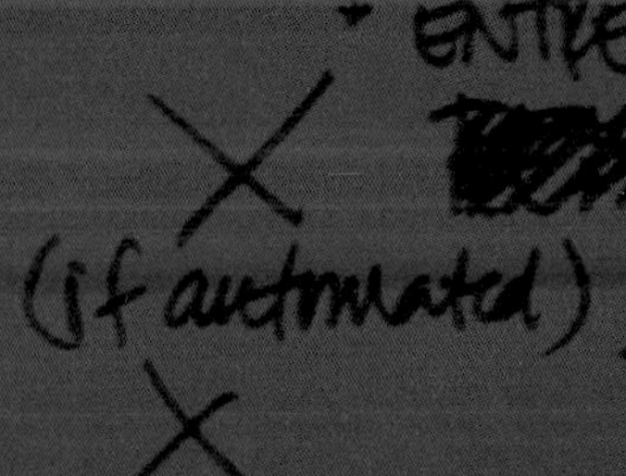

PLAN A PIPELINE OF SOLUTIONS

To understand how new solutions will move and grow your organization, map each solution to the matrix provided. As you are mapping solutions, ask whether each solution is targeted at your current customer group or whether it expands the group of customers you serve.

WATCH OUT

Existing users refers to the category of customers, such as people earning $1-2 per day vs. people earning greater than $2 a day, not those earning $1-2 per day who are current customers of your organization vs. people earning $1-2 per day who are not yet customers.

Determine whether the solutions extend or adapt an existing offer, or create a new offer. Analyze this information from the context of your investment strategy, mission, priorities and appetite for risk. Also identify which solutions fit naturally into programs already underway within your organization.

TIP #1

Many organizations say they are only looking for Revolutionary ideas, but their capabilities are limited to Incremental or Evolutionary ideas. Furthermore, funders can steer grantees toward more incremental ideas or ones that have been proven to be best practices. Make sure you are honest with how far your organization can stretch its capabilities and how willing your funders are to take risks. Mapping a pipeline of solutions that includes Incremental, Evolutionary, and Revolutionary ideas helps ensure that your design effort will pay off.

TIP #2

Remember, sometimes the ideas with the highest impact are the simple Incremental ideas.

Facilitator Notes

Time:
30-45 mins.

Difficulty:
★★☆☆☆

Step 1: Draw the matrix on a large sheet of flip-chart paper.

Step 2: Write each solution on a post-it note and place in the appropriate position on the matrix.

Step 3. Analyze if the team is happy with the distribution of solutions from Incremental to Revolutionary.

Step 4. If the team wants to add solutions to one of the quadrants, develop a HMW...? statement and brainstorm new solutions.

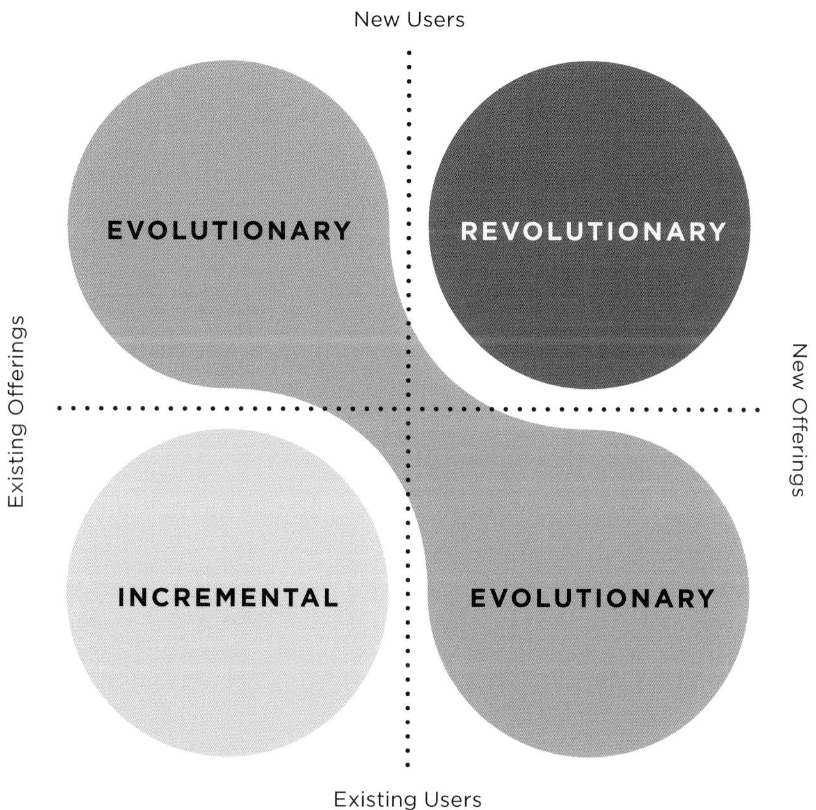

The lower left quadrant represents Incremental innovation as these solutions build on existing offerings with familiar users. Evolutionary innovation is about extending into either new offerings or new users while holding the other constant. Revolutionary innovation means tackling both new users and new offerings.

TIP #3

Look at the spread of solutions to reveal the gaps in your pipeline of solutions. Are parts of the matrix blank and others full? If so, determine if it is desirable for your organization to go back to Brainstorming in order to develop solutions that will intentionally fill that gap.

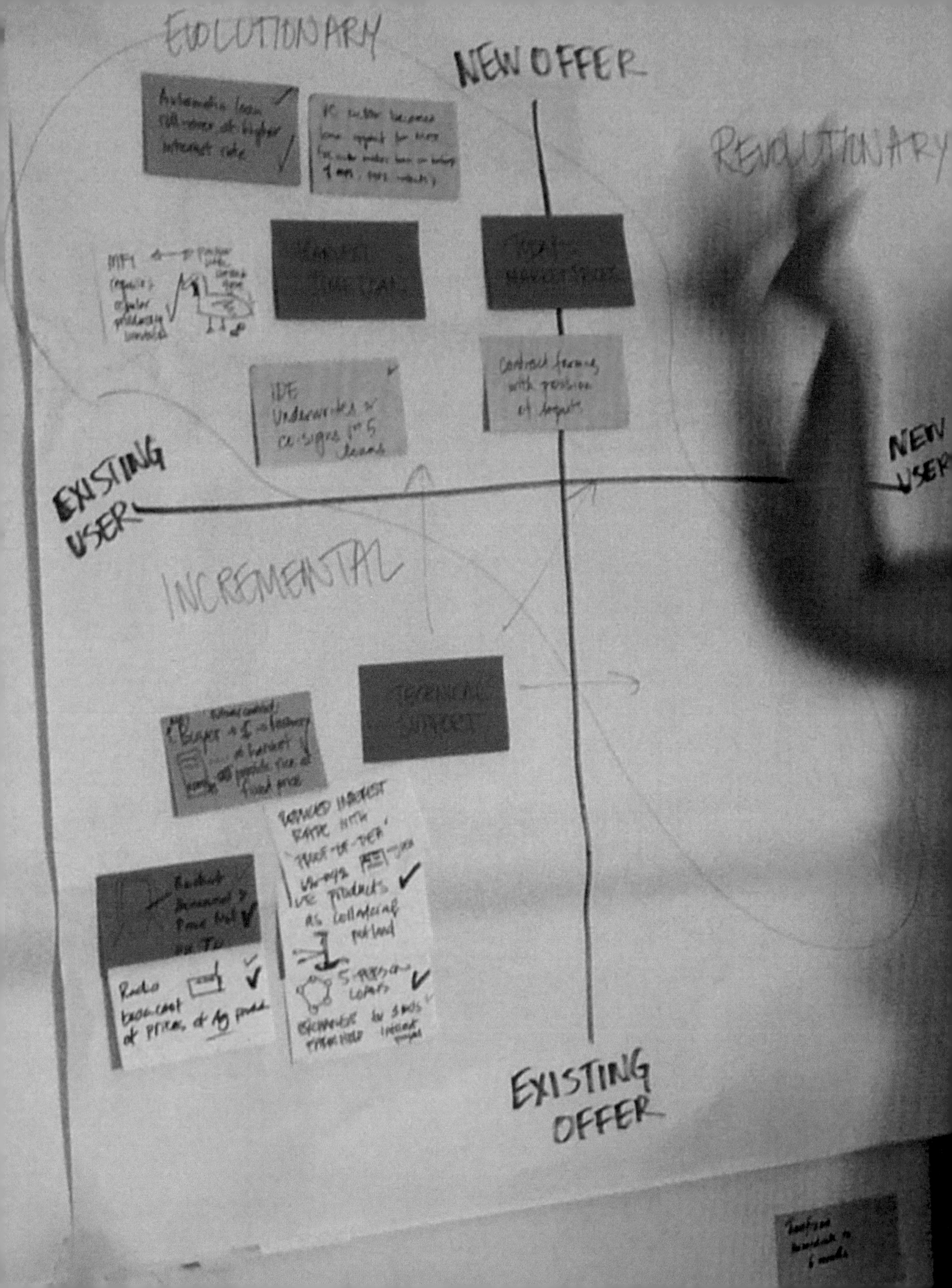

EVOLUTIONARY

NEW OFFER

REVOLUTIONARY

Automatic loan rollovers at higher interest rate

Contract farming with provision of inputs

IDE underwrites & co-signs 1st 5 loans

EXISTING USER

NEW USER

INCREMENTAL

TECHNICAL SUPPORT

Radio broadcast of prices at Ag (?)

EXISTING OFFER

CASE STUDY

CREATING A SOLUTIONS PIPELINE

In Cambodia, the IDE design team noticed that most of the solutions fell on the "existing user" side of the matrix since the organization has a highly defined target group. Yet the solutions spanned the range from those that fit within current projects and programs to new areas of offerings. The team also identified solutions that would start in the lower left corner with adaptations to existing solutions with existing customers, but over time would help the organization migrate into the other quadrants. While many organizations are initially attracted to the idea of "Revolutionary" innovations, in reality an innovation pipeline that focuses on existing capabilities or targets existing customers can be the strongest strategy for the near term.

CREATE AN IMPLEMENTATION TIMELINE

Map solutions to a timeline of implementation, with those in the Incremental innovation category early in the timeline and Revolutionary innovations further out.

Look at relationships of solutions to see whether initiating one solution will build the relationships and partners needed for another solution. You may also need to take into account which solutions can be explored within the scope of currently funded programs and which solutions suggest the proposal of new grants.

Facilitator Notes

Time:
15-30 mins.

Difficulty:
★★☆☆☆

Step 1: Create post-it notes for a timeline (such as 2 weeks, 1 months, 3 months, 6 months, 1 year) and post them along a large blank wall in your office.

Step 2: Post the Feasibility Assessments or post-it notes for each solution along the timeline.

Step 3. Assign champions to pursue the next steps.

Assigning an individual within your organization as a champion for each solution will help maintain momentum and increase the likelihood of implementation.

Divide each solution into a series of steps that build toward implementing the final solution. Challenge the team to do something toward implementing each solution in the next two weeks. For some solutions, a pilot can be launched in two weeks. For others, two weeks might be the amount of time required for further study or for the first steps to connecting with partners.

2 WEEKS
1 MONTH
3 MONTHS
6 MONTHS
1 YEAR

PLAN MINI-PILOTS & ITERATION

For each solution in your pipeline, it is important to identify simple, low-investment next steps to keep the ideas alive. One way to keep iterating and learning is to plan mini-pilots before large-scale pilots or full-scale implementation.

For each mini-pilot, ask three questions:

» What resources will I need to test out this idea?

» What key questions does this mini-pilot need to answer?

» How will we measure the success of this mini-pilot?

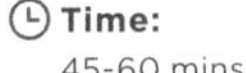

Facilitator Notes

Time:
45-60 mins.

Difficulty:
★★★☆☆

Step 1: Get into small groups per solutions and fill out the worksheet on the next page.

Step 2: Cross-share mini-pilot plans with the team and give each other feedback.

Step 3. Identify who will enact the most immediate next steps and establish the first check-in date.

GENDER

When planning mini-pilots, pilots, and implementation plans, it often makes sense to understand how these may differ by gender. By understanding these differences early on, the solution can be iterated or transformed to make sure that the roles and needs of both men and women are being appropriately addressed. For example, in planning the mini-pilot, consider how women's roles in implementation might differ from men's. For each solution, ask how women could play a role as:

» client
» resource
» beneficiary
» partner

Do any of the answers differ in the ways women would play these roles versus men? If so, iterate your solution to incorporate this finding.

TRY

Use the Mini-pilot worksheet to plan next steps for each solution.

After each mini-pilot, it is important to reconvene the design team to understand what went well and where there was customer dissatisfaction or system obstacles. Use the worksheet provided to continuously iterate the mini-pilots, trials, and success measures.

See the full-size worksheet on the next page.

MINI-PILOT WORKSHEET

MINI-PILOT PLANNING WORKSHEET

SOLUTION NAME:

TEAM MEMBERS:

» CONTEXT (WHO, WHERE, WHEN) & TIME
What's a low-cost, low-investment way to try out this solution? What can you do in 2 weeks?

» RESOURCES:
What resources (people, funds, permissions) would you need to try this out?

» QUESTIONS TO ANSWER:
What key questions do you have about this concept and its desirability for your customer?

» HOW TO MEASURE SUCCESS:
How will you know if your solution was successful? Successful for whom?

CHECK-IN DATE	CHECK-IN DATE	CHECK-IN DATE
» KEY LEARNINGS:	» KEY LEARNINGS:	» KEY LEARNINGS:
» NEW RESOURCES:	» NEW RESOURCES:	» NEW RESOURCES:
» NEW QUESTIONS:	» NEW QUESTIONS:	» NEW QUESTIONS:
» NEW MEASURES:	» NEW MEASURES:	» NEW MEASURES:

CREATE A LEARNING PLAN

Throughout the design and implementation of new solutions, it is important to keep learning. With Human-Centered Design, design and evaluation are one seamless process, since both require attention to the effects of solutions on the lives of people.

Early in the design process, you collected stories that helped develop the understanding to get you to new ideas. After the first ideas were prototyped, you gathered feedback to make those ideas better.

As implementation begins, it is important to keep learning about how the solutions are working in order to keep making the designs better, and to select how to spend valuable resources on the solutions that are making the most impact. Instead of thinking that implementation is when design ends and monitoring and evaluation activities begins, try to marry design and evaluation.

When ideas are implemented, the team should continue to collect stories and gather feedback from users. Stories collected from people in the Hear phase will help the team create a baseline to track how solutions are affecting individuals' lives. Collecting on-going feedback will help the team iterate on the ideas in order to make them more effective, more appropriate, and more cost-effective.

In addition to stories and feedback, begin to track indicators and outcomes. This is possible after the solutions are implemented and are important to measuring the impact as well as the return on investment of solutions.

Refer to 'Impact Planning and Learning Approaches' from Keystone at keystoneaccountability.org.

Refer to 'The Evaluation Toolkit' published by FSG at fsg-impact.org/ideas.

Facilitator Notes

Time:
45-60 mins.

Difficulty:
★★★☆☆

Step 1: Revisit the stories you gathered in the Hear phase as a baseline. Answer the questions: What was the situation of the people in our initial research? What should we expect to see happen in the lives of these people if our ideas are successful?

Step 2: Develop an approach to collect more stories of before, during, and after implementation. If possible, identify a demographically similar group that will not be affected by your ideas and collect their information as well for a robust study.

Step 3. Create a strategy for integrating qualitative and quantitative methods for learning.

Step 4: Encourage the team to embrace measurement as a process to enable on-going learning and inspire new solutions and pose new design challenges.

STORIES

- Assess Needs
- Understand Context
- Develop Baseline
- Gain Inspiration

FEEDBACK

- Evaluate Ideas
- Prioritize Solutions
- Iterate Ideas
- Develop Implementation Plan

INDICATORS

- Track Progress
- Choose Ideas
- Iterate Solutions
- Identify Unintended Consequences

OUTCOMES

- Assess Impact
- Evaluate ROI
- Create New Baselines
- Identify Next Challenges

THE LEARNING LOOP

Stories, feedback, indicators, and outcomes are all ways of gathering empirical data in order to learn. A project in India for clean water storage and transportation utilized all of these methods to measure the impact potential and outcomes of solutions.

METHOD: TRACK INDICATORS

Indicators help you measure the effects of your solutions. These effects can be positive or negative. They can also be intended or unintended.

Facilitator Notes

Time:
2-3 Hours

Difficulty:
★★★★☆

Step 1. Ask the team to refer back to the Theory of Change and to your holistic impact assessment stakeholder map.

Step 2. Focus on each stakeholder and/or step and for each one, list the information you would like to learn. For example, if the solution is focused on increasing women's income opportunities and the men in the community are a stakeholder, you might want to know how the solution is affecting the incomes and time allocations of both men and women.

Step 3. For each stakeholder and/or step, ask: Are there leading indicators we should be tracking? Are there analogous indicators we can track? How can we measure awareness and engagement? How will we track and understand the dynamics of transformation that are occurring?

Step 4. If possible, include constituents and other stakeholders directly in this process.

TYPES OF INDICATORS

Leading

The impact of solutions can often take some time to become evident, such as months or years. In these cases, it makes sense to track leading indicators. For example, if your goal is to reduce the number of unwanted pregnancies (an effect that will take at least nine months to see), a leading indicator would be adherence to birth control. If your goal is to increase farmer income, a leading indicator would be the number of farmers growing high-value crops this season.

Analogous

Sometimes it is difficult to see direct impacts. This is especially true when your design challenge is about trust or prevention. In these cases, try to find an indicator that would logically lead you to conclude whether your goal is being met. For example, on a project to increase trust of healthcare providers, the team tracked the number of questions people asked doctors and nurses. Since trust is hard to measure, the team decided to use the posing of questions as an analogous indicator of trust.

Awareness

When the goal involves people engaging or adopting something new, the first step is to know whether they are aware of the solution or design. Measuring awareness is a good early indicator to help understand how big the impact of the solution may be.

Engagement

Like awareness, measuring the number of people who are engaged in a new program is often very meaningful. For example, if the goal is to increase women's incomes through a program to export local art, the number of women actively seeking out and participating in the program is a meaningful indication of how much impact the program may have on local incomes.

Dynamic Changes

When a new solution is introduced, it is important to track the changes over time that occur within the community, within households, and to the environment. These shifts can be completely unexpected, and are sometimes positive and sometimes negative. Its crucial to lookout out for these changes and unintended consequences early on in implementation.

WATCH OUT

Often teams look for only the positive and intended consequences. To get a full view of impact, it is critical to challenge yourself to look for the negative and unintended consequences of solutions.

TIP #1

Ask yourself what you would expect to see happening if the solutions were improving the lives of people. For example, if your goal was to increase household income, would women starting more businesses be an early indicator? If your goal was to increase childhood vaccinations, would the number of casual conversations about vaccines be a possible indicator?

TIP #2

It is critical to track the effects of solutions on men and women, young and old, empowered and disempowered – even if your ideas are focused on other groups. Often the group that is not the intended audience for the solutions is a key player in the implementation and use of solutions.

Facilitator Notes

Time:
1-2 Hours

Difficulty:
★★★☆☆

Step 1. Evaluation has many stakeholders, including constituents, community leaders, government officers, funders, and others. When developing a plan to evaluate outcomes and impact, engage as many of these stakeholders as possible in the creation of your evaluation and learning plan. What will success look like from these multiple perspectives?

Step 2. Have the team discuss various qualitative and quantitative measurement methods. Refer to methods that have been tried as best practices, and brainstorm new methods that might be necessary to achieve your specific goals. Which of these are appropriate for the challenge? Which of these methods speak to the interests and goals of the different stakeholders?

Step 3. Develop a plan that includes the right mix of qualitative and quantitative methods that will help the team keep learning about how to improve upon solutions and how to deliver those solutions more effectively.

METHOD: EVALUATE OUTCOMES

Measuring outcomes is critical to the learning cycle. Without a good assessment of the impact a solution has made, there is often not enough information about the direction or goals for the next round of designs.

Assessing outcomes is important for everyone – the implementer, the funder, the design team, and the community. Outcome measurement helps people understand where to best invest their resources. It is an opportunity to assess and plan for the future.

WATCH OUT

Outcome evaluation should not be a hurdle to the implementers, grantees, or design team. By viewing this phase as a continuation of design and opportunity for learning, outcome measurement can be a rewarding experience for everyone.

TIP

The measurement process is iterative – return to stories and feedback based on learnings from quantitative measurements, and use stories and feedback to discover which variables to include in quantitative studies.

TRY #1

Use evaluation results as an opportunity for reflection and creation of new design challenges.

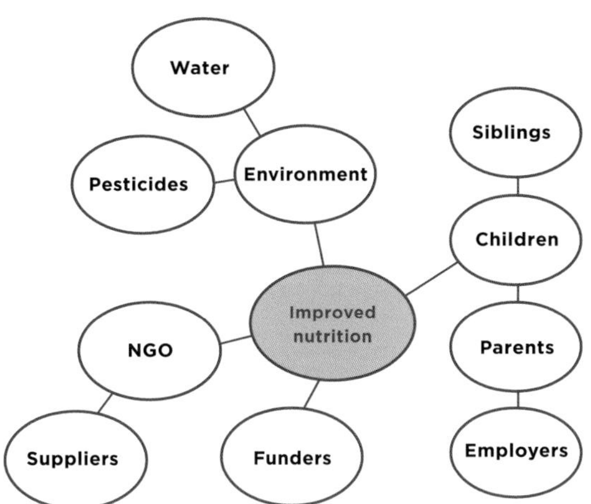

TRY #2

HOLISTIC IMPACT ASSESSMENT
To assess the impact of a solution, program, or intervention, it is important to take a systemic and holistic view. Try the following exercise, or develop a method of your own.

1. Map or list all the stakeholders that your solution might touch - in positive, negative, or neutral ways. Try to create a complete list with many actors. A mind map format works well for this exercise. Remember to include stakeholders that your team may not be focused on, such as: funders, people in the same community or adjacent communities who are not receiving direct benefits, and non-human stakeholders such as animals, the environment, and natural resources. Put this map or list in a place where you can refer to it often.

2. As you see and track the effects of a solution, write the effects on the list or map. Color code the actors that receive benefits from the solution and those that experience negative effects. If possible, quantify the value of the effects with a standardized measurement system.

3. Using this learning, continue to iterate on the solutions to find ways to increase the positive effects and lessen negative effects.

4. Examine the solution's net value Use this exercise as a way to continue learning and challenge the team to improve on solutions in order to make the outcomes more and more positive.

Facilitator Notes

Time:
1-2 Hours

Difficulty:
★★☆☆☆

Step 1. List the different stakeholders in the system or develop a map. To develop a mind map, first write the name of the solution on a large poster or board.

Step 2. Draw a line from the solution to the primary stakeholders who will be affected by the solution.

Step 3. From each primary stakeholder, draw a line and list the secondary stakeholders that will be affected by the solution.

Step 4. Keep going by mapping more and more stakeholders, including human and non-human stakeholders. When you are finished, have the team assess which of the stakeholders might be better off as a result of the solution, and which might be negatively affected.

Step 5. Develop methods and techniques to measure the impact on the stakeholders who might be both positively and negatively affected.

Step 6. Hang the map in a place where people can refer to it often. Capture thoughts and learnings in a section of the map so that it becomes a living document for helping the team learn and engage in discussion.

REESE
Opens
Why

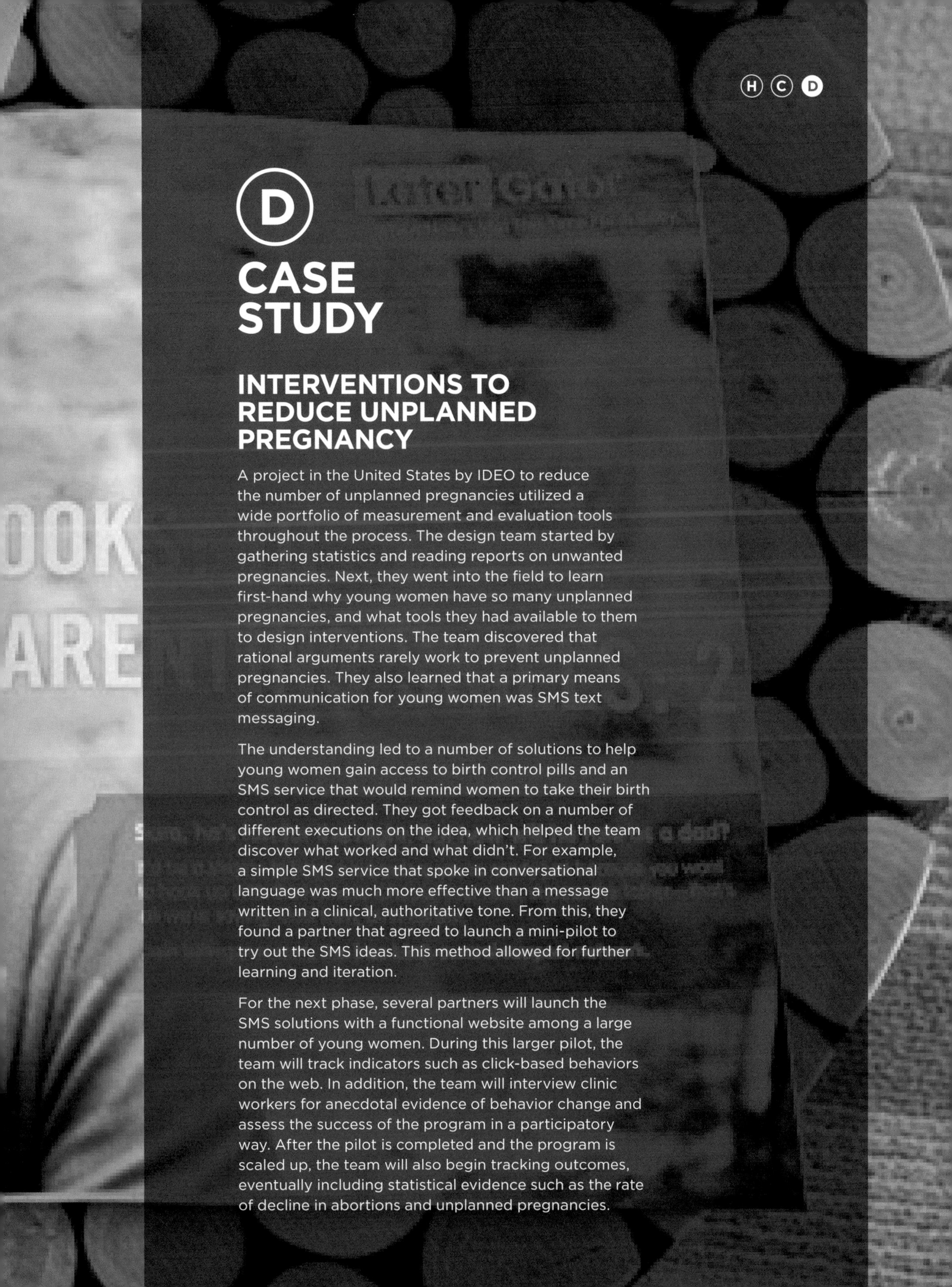

H C D

D

CASE STUDY

INTERVENTIONS TO REDUCE UNPLANNED PREGNANCY

A project in the United States by IDEO to reduce the number of unplanned pregnancies utilized a wide portfolio of measurement and evaluation tools throughout the process. The design team started by gathering statistics and reading reports on unwanted pregnancies. Next, they went into the field to learn first-hand why young women have so many unplanned pregnancies, and what tools they had available to them to design interventions. The team discovered that rational arguments rarely work to prevent unplanned pregnancies. They also learned that a primary means of communication for young women was SMS text messaging.

The understanding led to a number of solutions to help young women gain access to birth control pills and an SMS service that would remind women to take their birth control as directed. They got feedback on a number of different executions on the idea, which helped the team discover what worked and what didn't. For example, a simple SMS service that spoke in conversational language was much more effective than a message written in a clinical, authoritative tone. From this, they found a partner that agreed to launch a mini-pilot to try out the SMS ideas. This method allowed for further learning and iteration.

For the next phase, several partners will launch the SMS solutions with a functional website among a large number of young women. During this larger pilot, the team will track indicators such as click-based behaviors on the web. In addition, the team will interview clinic workers for anecdotal evidence of behavior change and assess the success of the program in a participatory way. After the pilot is completed and the program is scaled up, the team will also begin tracking outcomes, eventually including statistical evidence such as the rate of decline in abortions and unplanned pregnancies.

HUMA
CENTE
DESIG
FIELD
GUIDE

H C D

HUMAN CENTERED DESIGN

FIELD GUIDE

2ND EDITION

INTRO:

FIELD CHECKLIST

This Field Guide brings together the tools you'll need to lead successful group meetings and individual interviews.

Included in the Guide are exercises to complete before going into the field, tips for successful interviews, and a place to capture highlights from the interviews while they are still fresh in your mind.

» COMPLETE THE FOLLOWING:

- ☐ Worksheet: Recruiting Plan
- ☐ Worksheet: Research Schedule
- ☐ Worksheet: Identity, Power & Politics

» FAMILIARIZE YOURSELF WITH:

- ☐ Tips: Observation
- ☐ Tips: Conversation
- ☐ Tips: Discussion Guide
- ☐ Tips: Documentation
- ☐ Exercise: Community Characters
- ☐ Exercise: Resource Flow
- ☐ Exercise: Factors & Forces
- ☐ Exercise: Journey Of An Offering
- ☐ Exercise: Aspirations

» BRING WITH YOU:

- ☐ Camera
- ☐ Video Camera (optional)
- ☐ Pens & Markers
- ☐ Gifts for participants (optional)

» TO DEBRIEF, FILL OUT:

- ☐ Highlights

WORKSHEET:

RECRUITING PLAN

Recruiting the right participants is critical to success. Remember to recruit extremes and balance ethnic, class, and gender considerations.

Keeping track of the people you speak with can also be challenging. Use the worksheets to help keep a list of who you have spoken with and who you plan to speak with next.

GENDER For female participants, interviewers may need permission from male family members or community leaders.

» GROUP MEETING LOCATIONS

Example Group Meeting Location:
Village 1: Ansoung Commune of Kg Trabek District
Unique Characteristic: Seasonal Flooding

Village 1: ____________________

Unique Characteristic: ____________________

Village 2: ____________________

Unique Characteristic: ____________________

Village 3: ____________________

Unique Characteristic: ____________________

» INDIVIDUAL PARTICIPANT TYPES:

Example Participant Types:
Successful Villager
Person struggling to survive
Large family with relatives in the city
Female headed household

Participant types:

- ☐ ____________________
- ☐ ____________________
- ☐ ____________________
- ☐ ____________________
- ☐ ____________________
- ☐ ____________________
- ☐ ____________________

WORKSHEET:

RESEARCH SCHEDULE

» TEAM LEADS	» DETAILS
2 Teams: Asha & Anand	2 groups of 10 participants / mixed gender
» ACTIVITY	**» DATE**
Village 1 Group Meeting	Example: 7 June / 8:00 - 10:00 (including setup)

There are many things to juggle when you're out in the field. The more you plan ahead of time, the more smoothly the process will go. However, be prepared to adjust quickly; for example, you might need to increase the number of facilitators if you show up and the group is twice as large as expected.

WORKSHEET:

IDENTITY, POWER & POLITICS

» RACE & ETHNICITY

Are ethnic, racial, and/or tribal distinctions important in this community?

How might these issues affect the research and design challenge?

How will you deal with these issues in research?

» GENDER

Do women and men have unequal status in this context?

What activities within and outside the household do men and women do differently?

How might gender inequality affect the research and design challenge?

How will you deal with these issues in research?

» CLASS & INCOME

Are communities divided along class or income lines?

How might income and class divisions affect the research and design challenge?

How will you deal with these issues in research?

» THE ELITE

Who are the political or economic elites in this context?

How might their influence affect the research or design challenge?

How will you mitigate the influence of elites in research?

» THE DISEMPOWERED

Are any groups of people disempowered in this community (i.e. landless, children, disabled, etc)?

How might the perspectives of these groups affect the research and design challenge?

How might the research take into account the perspectives of the disempowered?

Research with communities and individuals often involves issues of identity, power, and politics. To help think through these issues, answer the questions above.

TIPS:

OBSERVATION

The things people say and what they actually do are often not the same thing. In-context observations are often useful for getting beyond what people say to understand what people do and feel.

In-context means being with people in their real settings, doing the things they normally do.

The stories that emerge from these encounters in the field show us new opportunities and inspire new solutions.

It is often very powerful to experience a process first-hand. Whenever possible, put yourself in the shoes of a customer and experience their activities directly.

For example:
» Work with a farmer for a day in his or her field.
» Live with a family for a few days.
» Go with a sick person to seek medical care.

TIP

During observations, look for:

» Things that prompt shifts in behavior

» Work-arounds and adaptations

» Body language

» Things people care about

» Anything that surprises you

» Anything that questions your assumptions about how the world works

» Anything that you find "irrational"

TIPS:

CONVERSATION

The in-context interview is a lengthy conversation (often 1.5+ hours) that explores the values, desires, frustrations, and aspirations of your interviewee. The conversation should:

Be long enough to make your interviewee feel like they are really being heard, and that allows them to go past their rehearsed "script"

Be focused enough so that you feel you are getting useful information to address your design challenge

Be general enough so that it feels like an open-ended conversation that can lead to unexpected insights

Generate a true back-and-forth so that it feels like a conversation and puts the interviewee at ease

Make the interviewee feel that the conversation is about them, not about the product, service, or organization you are representing

TIP

- **Ask open-ended questions, or questions that require a longer explanation than one word.**
- **Listen and be attentive, even if taking notes at the same time**
- **Have a dynamic conversation, don't interview from a script**
- **Allow long pauses**
- **Ask naïve questions (even if you're the expert) to hear the explanation in their words**
- **Don't correct people; understand their perceptions and why they may perceive things differently than you**
- **Remember: the participant is the expert!**

TIPS:

DISCUSSION GUIDE FOR FARMING

» OPEN SPECIFIC

Start the conversation with simple and specific questions your participants will feel comfortable answering. You may want to begin with a compliment and short introduction and then move on to questions about the participant's current life. This is your chance to build rapport with the person you are interviewing and to ask basic questions that will help you understand their overall life situation, the make-up of their household, and their farming activities.

» GO BROAD

Prompt bigger more general topics that ask the participant to think about life, business, and the future. Ask about their hopes and dreams for the future, as well as the barriers to achieving their goals. This is the chance to understand how they want to change their lives, what is standing in their way, and what they perceive the real paths to a better future might be.

» PROBE DEEP

Ask deeper questions about the design challenge at hand & prompt with 'what if' scenarios. The last half of the interview is the time to ask questions that are focused on your design challenge. Make sure to ask concrete questions of the participant that will help you define what is and is not desirable to this person.

EXAMPLE INTERVIEW GUIDE

» OPEN SPECIFIC

1. Farm demographics
   How many people live on your farm?
   Can you give me a tour of your farm?

2. Stories of recent past
   How did this year's harvest compare to last year's?
   Do you expect next year to be better or worse?

3. What do different members of the household do?
   What activities do women & men do differently?

» GO BROAD

4. Aspirations for the future - use Aspiration Cards
   Choose 3 cards that represent what you hope for your future.
   What did you choose and why?

5. System-based questions - use Factors & Forces worksheet
   The innermost circle represents your household.
   The middle circle your community.
   The outermost circle the nation and the world.
   What factors in each of these circles affect your prosperity?

6. Household (or Community) Resource Flow — use the worksheets to illustrate or write household revenues and expenditures.

7. Who do you turn to for information on farming and marketing your products? In your community? Outside the community? Who do you trust the most? Who gives you the best information?

» PROBE DEEP

8. Questions specific to innovation challenge (i.e Perceptions of Credit and Risk) Under what circumstances do people in your community take credit or loans? Have you ever taken credit? What for or why not?
   What was a recent, significant purchase? - Journey of an Offering Worksheet If you were offered a loan of $500, what would you do?

9. Sacrificial Concepts
   Create 1 possible future product, service or agreement options for them to react to. It's good to be provocative.

TIPS:

DISCUSSION GUIDE FOR HEALTH

» OPEN SPECIFIC

Start the conversation with simple and specific questions your participants will feel comfortable answering. You may want to begin with a compliment and short introduction and then move on to questions about the participant's current life. This is your chance to build rapport with the person you are interviewing and to ask basic questions that will help you understand their overall life situation, the make-up of their household, and their farming activities.

» GO BROAD

Prompt bigger more general topics that ask the participant to think about life, business, and the future. Ask about their hopes and dreams for the future, as well as the barriers to achieving their goals. This is the chance to understand how they want to change their lives, what is standing in their way, and what they perceive the real paths to a better future might be.

» PROBE DEEP

Ask deeper questions about the design challenge at hand & prompt with 'what if' scenarios. The last half of the interview is the time to ask questions that are focused on your design challenge. Make sure to ask concrete questions of the participant that will help you define what is and is not desirable to this person.

EXAMPLE INTERVIEW GUIDE

» OPEN SPECIFIC

1. Home Setup
   How many people live in your home?
   What do different members of your household do?

2. Home activities
   What is a day like in your home?
   What kind of things do adults and children do differently?
   Women and men?

3. Context, values
   How is life for you/your family/your community the same or different than it was last year?

» GO BROAD

4. Aspirations for the future – use Aspiration cards
   Choose 3 cards that represent what you hope for your future.
   What did you choose and why?

5. Inividual (or Household) Health Flow – use the worksheet
   Use the worksheet to illustrate or write what contributes to or takes away from that person's health.

6. System-based questions – use Factors and Forces worksheet
   The innermost circle represents your household.
   The middle circle your community.
   The outer circle, the nation and the world.
   What factors in each of these circles affect your health?

7. Who is the healthiest person/household in your community? Why?
   Who is the least healthy? What can/should be done for them to be more healthy? When you have questions about health, how do you find the answer? Where do you find the best information?

» PROBE DEEP

8. Questions specific to the innovation challenge, e.g. perceptions of vaccines, choices around cost/value of doctor visits for different ailments.
   Has anyone in your household needed to see a doctor recently?

9. Sacrificial concepts
   Create possible future product, service, or agreement options for them to react to. Use your assumptions and questions to generate sacrificial ideas. Keep it simple; the more it's just about one idea the better.

TIPS:

DOCUMENTATION

Capture everything you see, hear, smell, feel, and taste during the observation. It's important to capture the experience to bring back with you to the office and to share with team members who were not present.

Document the conversation with notes, photos, and/or recordings. In addition to your Field Guide, bring a digital camera and, if possible, a video camera or voice recorder.

Write down first interpretations of what's going on at the moment it happened; this critical information is often lost and difficult to remember later.

Immediately after the interview (or within 24 hours), jot down immediate big picture takeaways from the conversation using the Highlights page. The longer you wait, the more details and specifics may be lost.

It's often helpful to work with a partner—one person responsible for leading the interview while the other is capturing and documenting. Compare the experiences,

perceptions, and interpretations of the two people, and feel free to switch roles every day or so.

TIP

When documenting capture:

» Personal details (famlly size, acreage, crops, diet, location)

» Direct, unfiltered quotes (and your immediate interpretations)

» The expressions and feelings of the person, not just their words

» Ways they interacted with others and things in the environment

» Things they care about most

» Moments or things that elicited emotional responses, positive or negative

EXERCISE:

COMMUNITY CHARACTERS

This exercise is good for:

» Group interviews

» Warming up the participants

» Identifying individuals you want to follow up with after the session (often the eyes, ears or mouth of the community)

» STEP 1:
Begin by saying you'd like to get to know the community better by understanding the different roles people in the community play.

» STEP 2:
Ask the group to identify a specific person who represents the **eyes & ears** of the community. You might need to qualify this with a definition (i.e. someone who is always looking outward beyond the community for new ideas to bring into the community). People may be reluctant to call out individuals, so remind them that there are many who play this role and you are simply looking for one example.

» STEP 3:
Ask the group to explain why this person is the **eyes & ears.** If possible, ask for a specific story that happened in the last month when the person played that role. Take notes in the appropriate box.

» STEP 4:
Repeat for **mouth, brain, heart** or whichever feel most relevant.

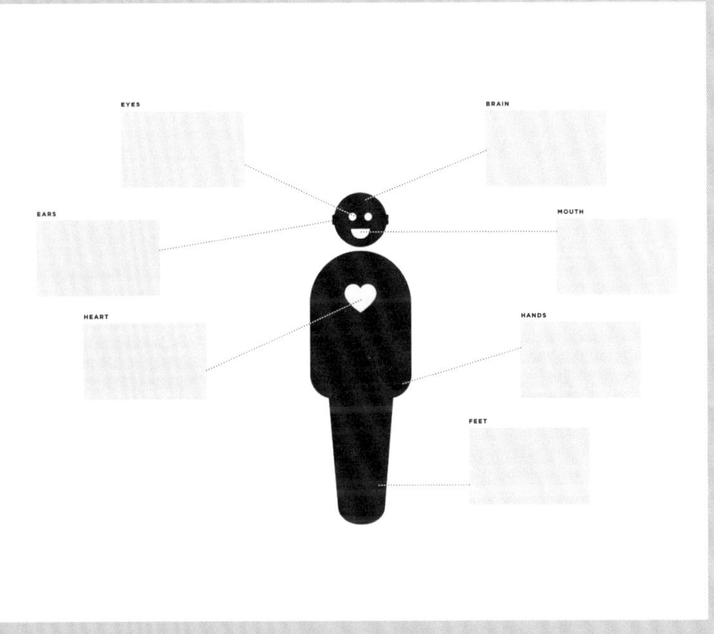

Community Characters Worksheet

GENDER

This activity works differently with mixed-gender, men-only or a women-only group.

If men are dominating in a mixed group, you may want to ask only the women to identify someone for a given role.

TIP

This can sometimes be a highly political activity, especially if there are community or government leaders present.

It's fine to abandon the exercise if the political environment is making this activity difficult.

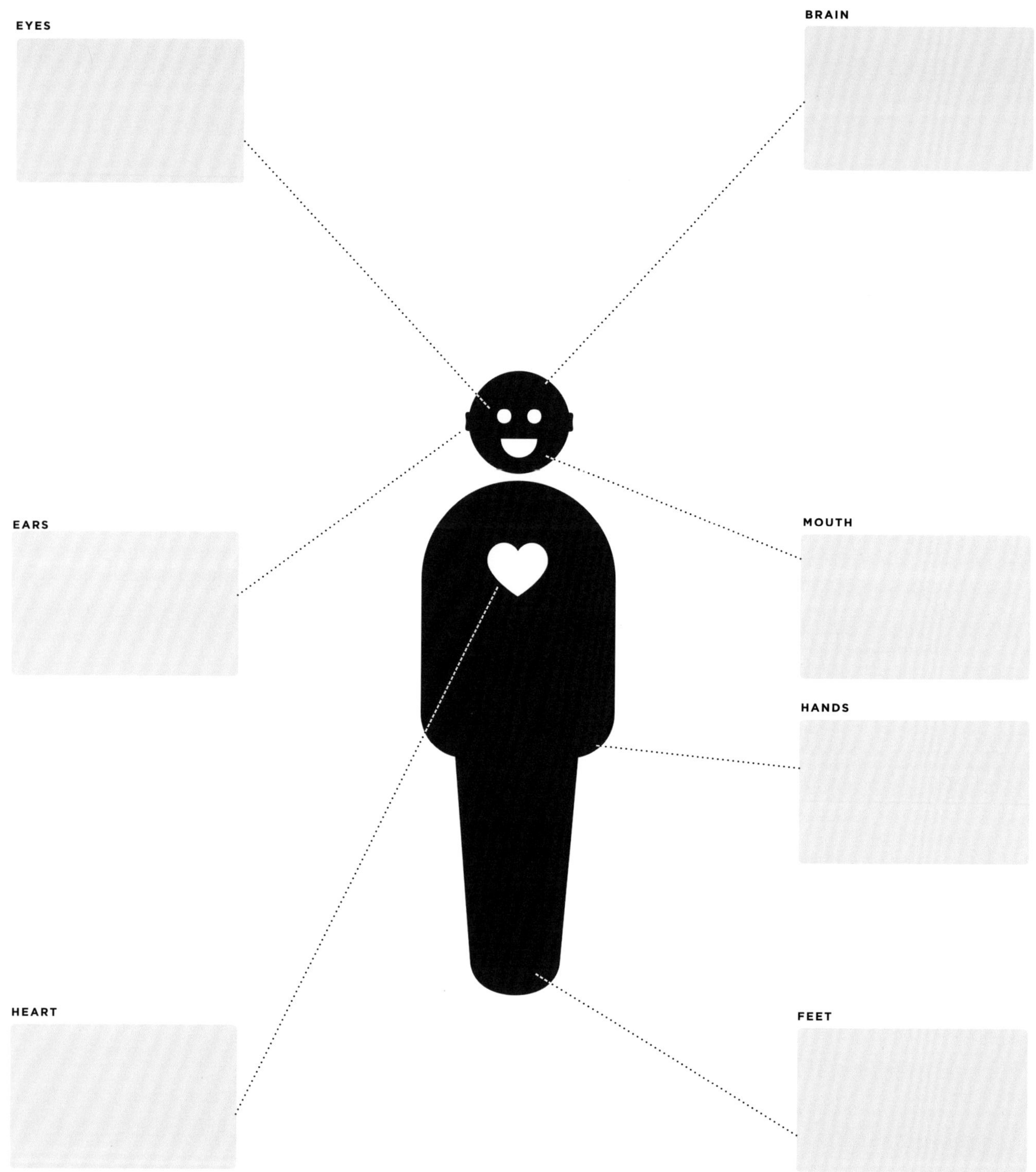
EYES
BRAIN
EARS
MOUTH
HANDS
HEART
FEET

EXERCISE:

RESOURCE FLOW

This exercise is good for:

» Group interviews

» Individual interviews

» FOR INDIVIDUAL INTERVIEWS:
Use Worksheet No. 2A

» STEP 1:
Ask if your participant or one of their children likes to draw. If not, it's fine for the participant or the interview leader to write.

» STEP 2:
Ask the participant to list everything that brings money INTO the household on the left side of the page. (This might include various crops, livestock, labor, etc)

» STEP 3:
Ask the participant to list everything that takes money OUT of the household on the right side of the page. (This might include seed, technology, education, medical expenses, etc)

» STEP 4:
Ask the participant to circle the item on the page that provides the largest income and the largest cost. Alternatively, you can ask them to rank order all the items listed.

» STEP 5:
Ask which items listed are controlled by the women and which are controlled by the men. Note this information down on the worksheet.

» FOR GROUP INTERVIEWS:
Use Worksheet No. 2B

» STEP 1:
Ask if anyone in the group likes to draw (often a teenager will volunteer). If no one volunteers, the interviewer can make notes based on what people say.

» STEP 2:
If someone voluteered to draw, ask that person to work with the group to draw representations of everything that bring money INTO the community on the left side of the page. (These means of income might include various crops, livestock, labor, etc)

» STEP 3:
Next, ask them to draw or say everything that takes money OUT of the community on the right side of the page. (These expenditures might include seed inputs, water technology, education, medical expenses, etc)

» STEP 4:
Ask them to circle the items on the page that provide the largest income and the largest cost.

» STEP 5:
If desired, ask them to rank all the items from most money to least money.

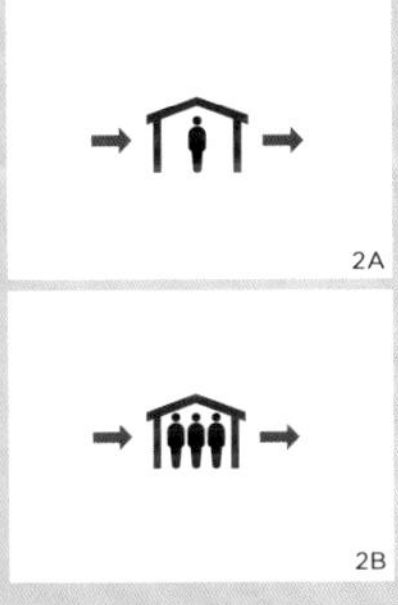

Resource Flow Worksheets

GENDER

Different cultures will often determine whether the man or the woman is in charge of decision-making and finances in the home. If one person is dominating the conversation, invite the input of the other. Sometimes it is helpful for the design team to split up into two groups—one to interview the husband and one to interview the wife. This enables you to cross-check and compare stories after the interview.

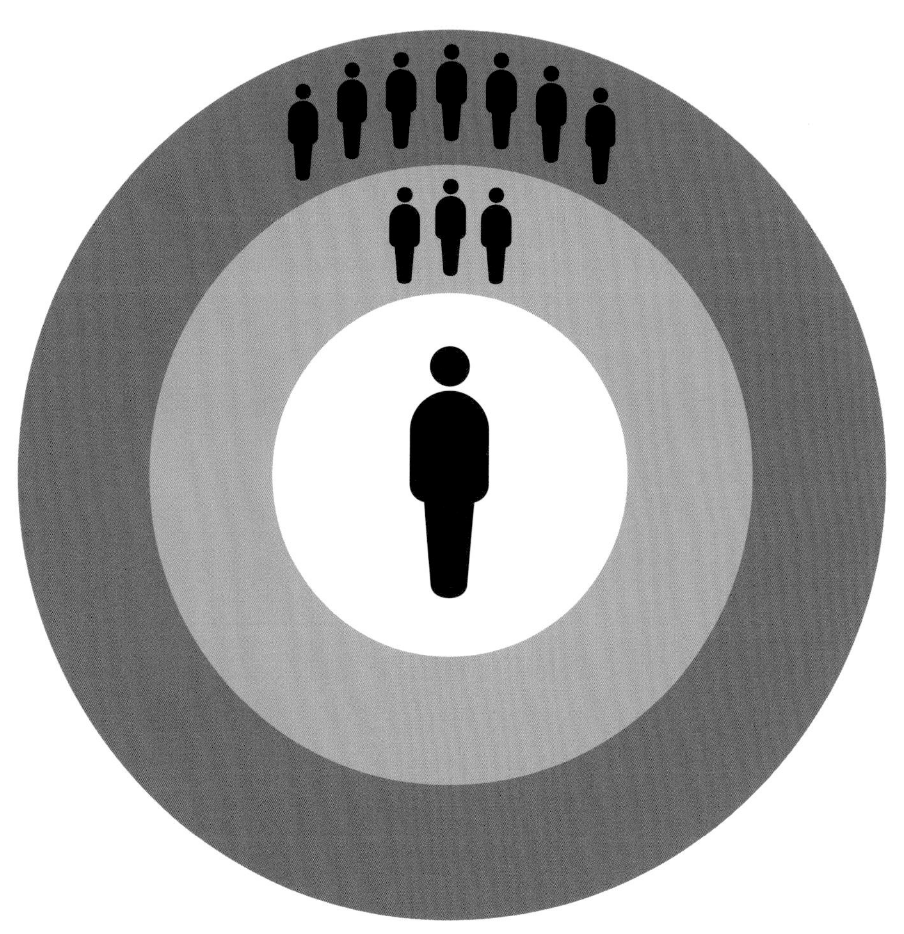

EXERCISE:

FACTORS & FORCES

GENDER

In mixed-gender group sessions, the women will stay quiet in some cultures though they have many ideas to share. When asking for responses to these questions, you might say "I'd like five people to respond to this question" and point to five people who represent a mix of genders.

Near the end of the exercise, ask what brings prosperity to the women of the community or household. Note if these factors are different.

This exercise is good for:

» Group Interviews

» Individual Interviews

» Broadening the conversation beyond one's immediate individual needs and circumstances

» Inviting conflicting opinions from different members of community for rich dialogue

» FOR GROUP INTERVIEWS:

» STEP 1:
Tell the group that you want to understand all the factors and forces that affect their prosperity.

Describe the diagram:
» The innermost circle is the community
» The second circle is the nation
» The third circle is the world

» STEP 2:
Ask what factors in the community, in the nation and in the world BRING prosperity to the community (i.e. health, work ethic, children in school, etc). Start with the community level and build outwards to the world. Take notes in the appropriate circles.

» STEP 3:
Ask what factors in the world, in the nation and in the community take prosperity AWAY from the community (i.e. violence, cost of fuel, legal status, property ownership, climate change, globalization, etc). Take notes in the appropriate circles.

» FOR INDIVIDUAL INTERVIEWS:

» STEP 1:
Tell your participant that you want to understand all the factors and forces that affect their prosperity.

Describe the diagram:
» The innermost circle is the person and his/her family
» The second circle is their community
» The third circle is their country and the world

» STEP 2:
Ask what factors in the family, in the community and in the nation BRING prosperity to their family. Start with the household level and build outwards to the nation. Take notes in the appropriate circles.

» STEP 3:
Ask what factors in the nation, in the community and in the household take prosperity AWAY from their family. Take notes in the appropriate circles.

Factors & Forces Worksheet

EXERCISE:

JOURNEY OF AN OFFERING

This exercise is good for:

» Individual interviews

» Understanding what a person considers when purchasing a new product or servicefor the first time

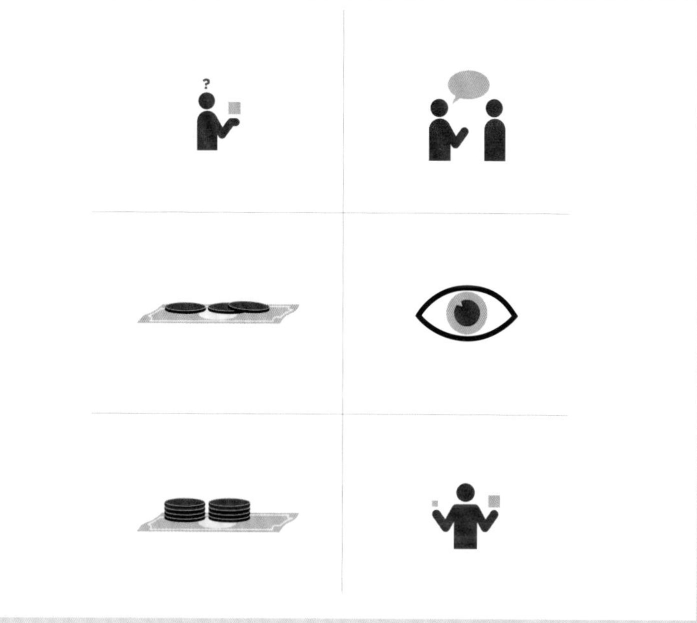

Journey of an Offering Worksheet

» STEP 1:
Tell the participant that you want to know what they think about when deciding to make a purchase.

» STEP 2:
Ask the participant to think of the last time they bought a new thing or service.

» STEP 3:
Show the participant the cards: talk, look, compare, try, money. Ask them to tell you how they did these things when making their purchase.

Talk: Did you talk to people about the product or service? Who and why? What were your questions? Did you talk to anyone about it after you made the purchase?

Look: Where did you see this product or service? What did you think at the time?

Compare: What other options did you consider? What else did you compare this to?

GENDER

Different cultures will often determine whether the man or the woman is in charge of decision-making and finances in the home. If the man is the dominant voice in the conversation, listen to his explanation first, then ask for the woman to describe the journey from her perspective.

Sometimes it is helpful for the design team to split up into two groups—one to interview the husband and one to interview the wife. This enables you to cross-check and compare stories after the interview.

TIP

This exercise can also be used to discuss a potential product or service.

TRY

COMPARE

SAVE

LOOK AT MARKET

GET CREDIT

TALK

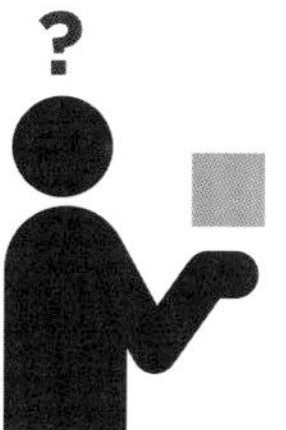

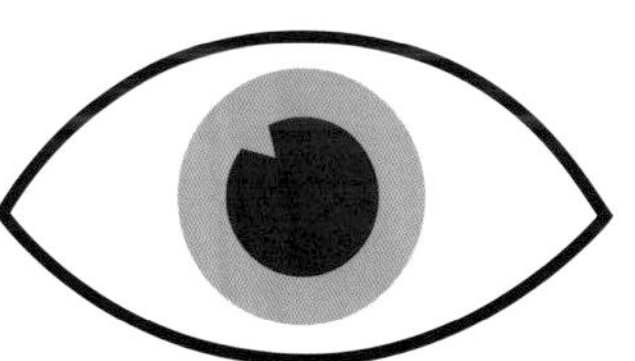

EXERCISE:

ASPIRATIONS EXERCISE

This exercise is good for:

» Engaging participants in group and individual interviews

» Getting people to talk about what they desire for the future

» Making people feel comfortable talking about broader issues

» STEP 1:
Start by saying that you want to know what the participants hope for and desire for the future.

» STEP 2:
Tell the participants that you have a set of cards with various pictures on them.

» STEP 3:
Ask the participants to look through the cards and choose the three pictures that represent what they hope for in the future.

» STEP 4:
If a participant asks, "what is this?" to a picture, tell them that it is anything they think it is, or if the picture doesn't make sense to them, skip it and move on.

» STEP 5:
After the participants have chosen their pictures, ask "Tell me what you chose" and have them describe the picture. Then ask: "Why did you choose this?" Document both the pictures and explanations.

Journey of an Offering Worksheet

TIP

Have the participants explain what the picture is in their own words, do not interpret the pictures for them. Often people will choose something that represents one thing to them, but may represent something different to the researcher.

TIP

If appropriate, you can ask people to choose the three pictures that represent what they fear in the future after they are finished with the first exercise.

TRY

You may find that you need different pictures for your design challenge or the community you are working with. With the help of the internet, find some pictures and print them out to add to this group of pictures.

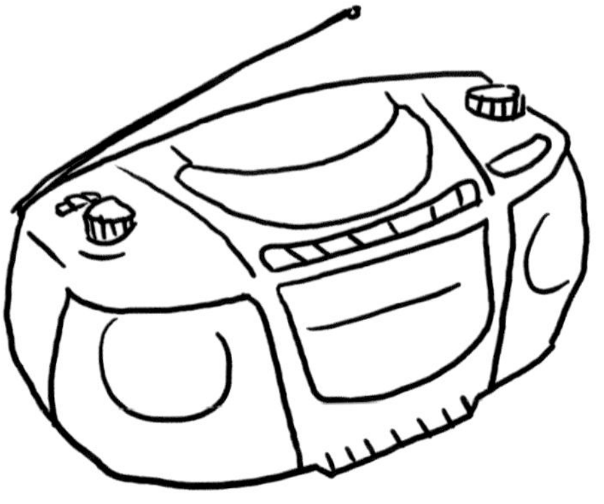

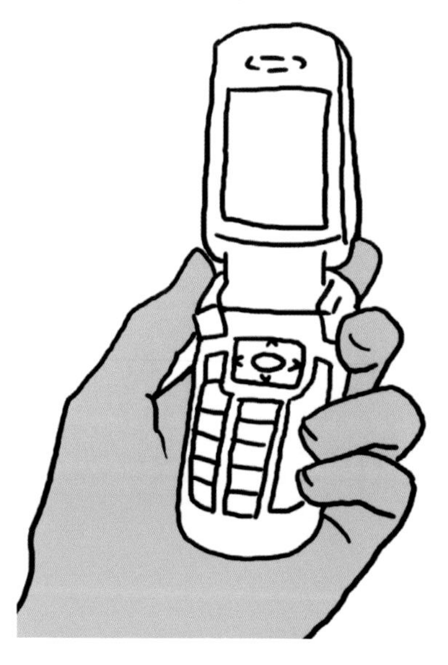

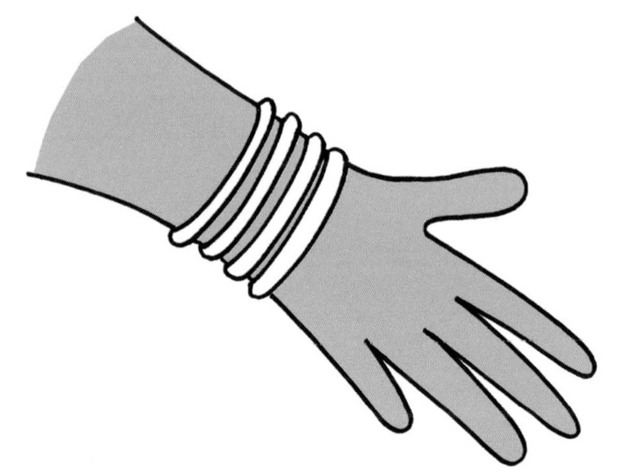

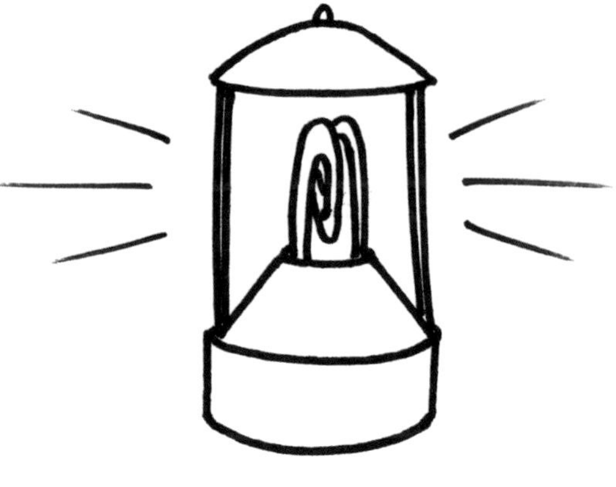

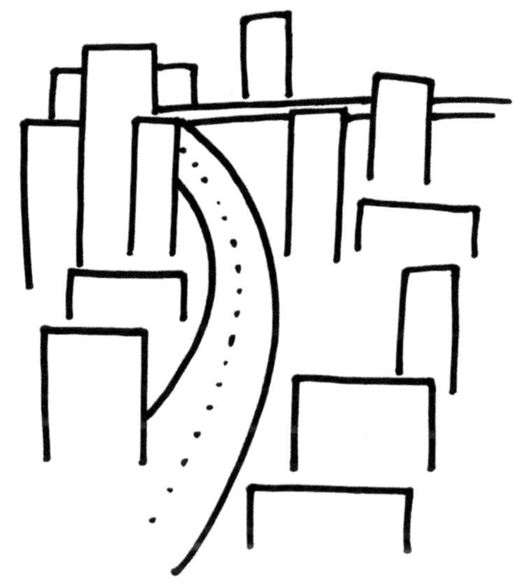

WORKSHEET:

HIGHLIGHTS

» DATE:

» NAME:

» LOCATION:

» TYPE OF ACTIVITY:

- ☐ Group Interview
- ☐ Individual Interview
- ☐ In-Context Immersion
- ☐ Other

THINGS THE PARTICIPANT(S) SAID OR DID THAT SURPRISED YOU OR MOST MEMORABLE QUOTES:

THINGS THAT MATTER MOST TO THE PARTICIPANT(S):

MAIN THEMES OR LEARNINGS THAT STOOD OUT FROM THIS INTERVIEW:

NEW TOPICS OR QUESTIONS TO EXPLORE IN FUTURE INTERVIEWS:

ACKNOWLEDGEMENTS

This Toolkit is the result of a project funded by the Bill & Melinda Gates Foundation. The BMGF brought together four organizations—IDEO, IDE, Heifer International, and ICRW—to partner in the creation of a method for guiding innovation and design for people living under $2/day.

As one of the key developers of the Human-Centered Design process, an IDEO team led the creation of this Toolkit. While IDEO takes responsibility for its shortcomings, we cannot take responsibility for any of its successes. These successes are the outcome of an extraordinary collaboration of partnerships on many continents—and the individuals that went above and beyond to prototype and field test these methods. Working on-site with IDE teams in Ethiopia, Zambia, Cambodia, Vietnam, and the US, as well as with Heifer International in Kenya, the HCD process was adapted for use with constituents in developing contexts.

IDEO revised and re-released the second edition of the Toolkit drawing on other social impact projects and on inspiration from outside users of the Toolkit.

Thanks to Kara Pecknold for sharing her use of the Human-Centered Design Toolkit in Rwanda as case study. Thanks also to Fidel Calderon and Indhira Rojas for the visual design of this edition. To add your own experiences or give feedback for the next edition of this Toolkit, email info@ideo.org

This is a working prototype.
Let's keep learning, adapting, and iterating together.